GENESIS

VOLUME II
CHAPTERS 16 - 33

by

J. Vernon McGee

THRU THE BIBLE BOOKS
Box 100
Pasadena, California 91109

First Printing
1975

Printed by
El Camino Press
LaVerne, California

CONTENTS

GENESIS — Volume II

PREFACE

These volumes on Genesis are transcribed and edited from the taped messages given on the five-year program of the Thru the Bible Radio Network.

For years I have taught both Bible institute and seminary students that the two key books of the Bible are Genesis and Matthew. Our messages in the five-year program on the book of Matthew have already been published. They have had a wide reception without much publicity and fanfare of trumpets. They were the pilot books in a series that we are hopeful will include the sixty-six books of the Bible.

This very ambitious program could not be accomplished without the able assistance of Dr. Dorothy Ritzmann and Dr. Leonard Ritzmann, a husband and wife team, with a corps of typists. There will be over one hundred volumes when all is accomplished.

Since Genesis is such an important book to the understanding of Scripture, we send these little books out into the sea of books with the hope and prayer that they might help some sailor on the sea of life to plot a direct course through Scripture; and by so doing be enabled to make a departure like Paul's on the sea of eternity, having finished his course down here *on course.*

Genesis is that important to the study of Scripture.

INTRODUCTION

The book of Genesis is one of the two important key books of the Bible. The book that opens the Old Testament, Genesis, and the book that opens the New Testament, Matthew, are the two books that I feel are the key to the understanding of the Scriptures.

The first thing I would like to suggest is that you read the book of Genesis through. It is preferable that you read it at one sitting. I realize it may be impossible for you to do this. To be truthful, I have never been able to read it at one sitting — it took me several sittings because of interruptions. But at least read it straight through from beginning to end in as short a time as possible.

Before we study Genesis chapter by chapter, we need a bird's eye view, a view that will cover the total spectrum of the book.

Genesis is the "seed plot" of the entire Scriptures. In the book of Genesis there is the origin of everything. All the great themes of Scripture can be found in Genesis. They are wrapped up like the bud of a flower and they open up in the light of the remainder of God's revelation. Genesis contains the beginnings of our created world, of man, woman, sin, sabbath, marriage, family, labor, civilization, culture, murder, sacrifice, races, languages, cities, and redemption.

You will find certain phrases occuring frequently. For instance, "these are the generations of" recurs often because the book of Genesis gives the families. This is important to us since we are members of the human family which begins here.

There are a number of very interesting characters whose lives are portrayed for us here. Someone has called it "the book of biographies." There are Abraham, Isaac, Jacob, Joseph, and the eleven other sons of old Jacob besides Joseph.

You will find it to be a book of blessings. God is continually blessing Abraham, Isaac, Jacob, and Joseph — also those who are associated with them are blessed. For instance, Lot, Abimelech, Potiphar, and Pharoah, all were blessed.

In this book you will find repeated mention of the covenant. There are frequent appearances of the Lord to the patriarchs, especially to Abraham. The altar is prominent in this book. Judgments upon sin are detailed in this book, and the wonderful leadings of providence. Problems in the home — marital relationships, child rearing, jealousy, deception, and hatred are found here.

As we study the book, we need to keep in mind something that Browning wrote years ago in a grammarian's funeral essay. "Image the whole, then execute the parts. Fancy the fabric, quiet, e'er you build, e'er steel strike fire from quartz, e'er mortar dab brick." In other words, get the total picture of the book. As a teacher of the Bible, I formerly would tell the students in my classes that there are two ways of studying the Bible. One is with the telescope and the other is with the microscope. At first you need the telescope. Get off at a distance and see all of it. After that, study it with a microscope, word by word.

A great man of the past, a great preacher of England, has written these words which I wish were indelibly written in the minds and hearts of God's people today:

> We live in the age of books. They pour out for us from the press in an ever increasing multitude. And we are always reading manuals, textbooks, articles, books of devotion, books of criticism, books about the Bible, books about the Gospels, all are devoured with avidity. But what amount of time and labor do we give to the consideration of the Gospels themselves? We're constantly tempted to imagine that we get good more quickly by reading some modern statement of truth which we find comparatively easy to appropriate because it is presented to us in a shape, and from a standpoint, with which our education, or it may be partly association, has made us familiar. But the good we acquire readily is not that which enters most deeply into our being and becomes an abiding possession. It would be well if we could realize quite simply that nothing worth the having is to be gained without the winning. The great truths of nature are not offered to us in such a form as to make it easy to

grasp them. The treasures of grace must be sought
with all the skill and energy which are characteristic
of the man who is searching for goodly pearls. (Robin-
son, *The Personal Life of the Clergy*.)

I love that statement because it has been true in my experience.
The Word of God speaks to our hearts as no other book can
speak.

MAJOR DIVISIONS OF THE BOOK

The first eleven chapters of Genesis constitute a whole. Then,
beginning with the eleventh chapter, through the twentieth
chapter, we find an altogether different section. It differs in
several ways.

The first section deals with major subjects which set the stage
for the human story. These subjects still engage the minds of
thoughtful men today.

Creation	Genesis 1 and 2
The Fall	Genesis 3 and 4
The Flood	Genesis 5 to 9
The Tower of Babel	Genesis 10 and 11

These four events furnish the key to most of the mysteries of life
about us.

The second section of the book has to do with personalities.

Abraham, the man of faith	Genesis 12 to 23
Isaac, the beloved son	Genesis 24 to 26
Jacob, the chosen and chastened son	Genesis 27 to 36
Joseph, suffering and glory	Genesis 37 to 50

The difference between the two sections — which, to my judgment, is major and really tremendous — is the difference in the
time span. The first eleven chapters cover a minimum time span
of 2,000 years — actually they may cover several hundred thousand years. I believe this first section of Genesis can cover any
time in the past that you need to fit into your theory. But at least
we know that the first section of the book covers a minimum of
2,000 years.

The second section, from Genesis 12 to 50, covers only 350 years. The beginning of the twelfth chapter of Genesis, going all the way through the Old Testament and the New Testament, spans 2,000 years. So, as far as time is concerned, my friend, when you cover the first eleven chapters in Genesis, you are half way through the Bible. The following chart may prove helpful.

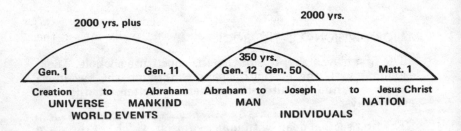

2000 yrs. plus   2000 yrs.

350 yrs.

Gen. 1   Gen. 11   Gen. 12   Gen. 50   Matt. 1

Creation   to   Abraham   Abraham   to   Joseph   to   Jesus Christ
UNIVERSE   MANKIND   MAN   NATION
WORLD EVENTS   INDIVIDUALS

God has something very definite in mind in giving this first section to us — we need some insight into the beginnings — but where do you think the emphasis lies? Is it not evident that He is putting the emphasis on the last part? The first section of Genesis furnishes an introduction to the remainder of Scripture. But the last part of Genesis is the story of one family. God was more interested in Abraham than He was in the entire created universe. And God, my friend, is more interested in you and attaches more value to you than He does to the entire physical universe.

Let me illustrate this with another example.

There are 89 chapters in the 4 Gospels:
4 chapters cover the first 30 years of the life of Jesus Christ;
85 chapters cover the last 3 years of His life;
27 chapters cover the last 8 days of His life.

Where is God putting the emphasis? I'm sure you will say the big emphasis is on the last part, the last eight days covered by the twenty-seven chapters. And what is that all about? It's all about the death, burial, and resurrection of the Lord Jesus Christ. That, my friend, is the important part of the Gospel record. In other words, God has given the Gospels that you might believe that Christ died for our sins and that He was raised for our justification. That is essential. That is the all-important truth.

May I say to you that the first eleven chapters of Genesis form the introduction to the Bible, and we need to look at it in that fashion. I'm of the opinion that if Moses were present today and heard all of the discussion about creation, for instance, and the record that he gave, and heard what the theologians and the scientists are saying, he'd be rather amused. I think that he would make the comment, "Well, all of you really missed the point. I wasn't attempting to give you the account of creation. I was simply giving you a few facts that would be the beginning, but that is not really my story. My story had to do with God dealing with man in sin. The story that I wanted to tell was the story of redemption. If you think that I was writing a scientific book on creation, you missed the entire point. I was writing a spiritual book on redemption." That is very important to see.

This does not mean we are going to pass over the first eleven chapters. We will spend quite a bit of time in them. Genesis is the seed plot of the Bible, and here we find the beginning, the source, the birth of everything. The truth given here is in germ form.

One way of considering the book of Genesis is according to the generations. This can be one way of making divisions in the book.

Gen. 1-2:6	Book of Generations of Heavens and Earth
Gen. 2:7-6:8	Book of Generations of Adam
Gen. 6:9-9:29	Generations of Noah
Gen. 10:1-11:9	Generations of Sons of Noah
Gen. 11:10-26	Generations of Sons of Shem
Gen. 11:27-25:11	Generations of Terah
Gen. 25:12-18	Generations of Ishmael
Gen. 25:19-35:29	Generations of Isaac
Gen. 36:1-37:1	Generations of Esau
Gen. 37:2-50:26	Generations of Jacob

The first division presents four outstanding events, while the second division presents four outstanding personalities.

WRITER

Genesis is the first of the five books of the Pentateuch. *Pentateuch* means "five books." These books were written by Moses, and are identified in Scripture as the Law. Although the Mosaic authorship has been questioned, it is affirmed by conservative scholars and confirmed by archaeology. Bible believers unanimously accept the Mosaic authorship (see Deuteronomy 31:9, 24, 26; Acts 7:37, 38).

RECOMMENDED BOOKS FOR FURTHER STUDY

There is a great deal of excellent material available on the book of Genesis. You will find it listed in the bibliography at the conclusion of this book.

OUTLINE

A. Entrance of Sin on Earth, chs. 1-11
  I. Creation, chs. 1, 2
    1. Heaven and Earth, 1:1
       "Create" (bara) occurs only 3 times, vv. 1, 21, 27.
    2. Earth Became Waste and Void, 1:2
    3. Re-creation, 1:3-2:25
      (1) First Day — Light, 1:3-5
      (2) Second Day — Air Spaces (Firmament), 1:6-8
      (3) Third Day — Dry Land Appears and Plant Life, 1:9-13
      (4) Fourth Day — Sun, Moon, Stars Appear, 1:14-19
      (5) Fifth Day — Animal Life (Biology), 1:20-23
      (6) Sixth Day — Fertility of Creation
         and Creation of Man, 1:24-31
      (7) Seventh Day — Sabbath, 2:1-3
      (8) Recapitulation of the Creation of Man, 2:4-25
         (law of recurrence)

  II. Fall, chs. 3, 4
    1. Root of Sin — Doubting and Disobeying God
    2. Fruit of Sin —
      "Out of the heart proceed ... murders ..." (Matt. 15:19)

  III. Flood (deluge), chs. 5-9
    1. Book of Generations of Adam — Through Seth
      Beginning of Man's History — Obituary Notices, ch. 5
    2. Antediluvian Civilization —
      Cause of Flood and Construction of Ark, ch. 6
    3. Judgment of Flood, ch. 7
    4. Postdiluvian Civilization — After the Flood, ch. 8
    5. Postdiluvian Life — New Beginning, ch. 9

IV. Tower of Babel and Confusion of Tongues, chs. 10, 11
1. Ethnology — Sons of Noah, ch. 10
2. Tower of Babel, ch. 11
   (contrast to Day of Pentecost)

B. Preparation for the Coming of the Redeemer of All Mankind, chs. 12-50
   I. Abraham (faith), chs. 12-23
      (development of faith by 7 appearances of God)
      1. God's Call and Promise to Abram —
         His Response by Lapse of Faith, ch. 12
      2. Abram Returns to Land from Egypt — Separates from Lot —
         God Then Appears the Third Time to Abram, ch. 13
      3. The First War — Abram Delivers Lot — The First Priest —
         Abram Blessed by Melchizedek, ch. 14
      4. God Reveals Himself More Completely
         to Abram — Reaffirms His Promises, ch. 15
      5. Unbelief of Sarai and Abram — Birth of Ishmael, ch. 16
      6. God Makes Covenant with Abraham
         (Abram Becomes Abraham) —
         Confirms Promise to Abraham About a Son, ch. 17
      7. God Reveals Coming Destruction of Sodom to Abraham —
         Abraham Intercedes on Behalf of Inhabitants, ch. 18
      8. Angels Warn Lot — Lot Leaves Sodom —
         God Destroys Cities of the Plain, ch. 19
      9. Abraham Repeats Sin
         at Gerar About Relationship of Sarah, ch. 20
      10. Birth of Isaac — Hagar and Ishmael Cast Out —
          Abraham at Beer-sheba, ch. 21
      11. God Commands Abraham to Offer Isaac — Restrains Him —
          Reconfirms Covenant with Abraham, ch. 22
      12. Death of Sarah — Abraham Purchases
          Machpelah Cave for Burial Place, ch. 23

   II. Isaac (the Beloved Son), chs. 24-26
       Choosing of a bride compares with Christ and the Church.
       1. Abraham Sends Servant for Bride for Isaac — Rebekah
          Returns With Him — Becomes Isaac's Bride, ch. 24

with Joseph — Leave Simeon as Hostage — Return
Home with Corn and Refunded Money, ch. 42

(3) Jacob Sends Sons (Benjamin Included) Again to
Egypt — Entertained in Joseph's Home
(Does Not Reveal His Identity), ch. 43

(4) Joseph Sends Brothers Home — Arrested by
Steward — Cup Found in Benjamin's Sack —
Judah Pleads for Benjamin, ch. 44

(5) Joseph Reveals Identity —
Tender Reunion with Brothers —
Invites Jacob and All Family to Egypt, ch. 45

(6) Jacob with Family (70) Move to Egypt —
Jacob and Joseph Reunited, ch. 46

(7) Jacob and Brothers Dwell in Goshen —
Presented to Pharaoh — Famine Forces Egyptians
to Sell Land to Joseph for Pharaoh —
Joseph Swears He Will Bury Jacob in Canaan, ch. 47

(8) Jacob on Deathbed Blesses Joseph's Sons, ch. 48

5. Death and Burial of Jacob and Joseph, chs. 49, 50

(1) Jacob Gives Deathbed Blessing
and Prophecy for Twelve Sons, ch. 49

(2) Death and Burial of Jacob in Canaan —
Death and Burial of Joseph in Egypt, ch. 50

CHAPTER 16

In this chapter we see another one of the tests of Abraham in which he failed. We see the unbelief of both Sarai and Abraham and the birth of Ishmael. Abraham had such a mountain peak experience in the preceding chapter, one would think he would really be treading on high places now. But we see that Abraham is not perfect. We see a lapse of his faith here. God's delay led Abraham to doubt; so he took matters into his own hands and attempted to assist God by an act of which God did not approve. This is really quite a let-down from the previous chapter.

SARAI'S SUGGESTION THAT ABRAHAM TAKE HAGAR, HER MAID

Now Sarai Abram's wife bare him no children: and she had an handmaid, an Egyptian, whose name was Hagar [Gen. 16:1].

Remember, we said that Abraham got two things down in the land of Egypt which really caused his troubles. The one cause of trouble was wealth and the other was this little Egyptian maid that he got down there.

And Sarai said unto Abram, Behold now, the LORD hath restrained me from bearing: I pray thee, go in unto my maid; it may be that I may obtain children by her. And Abram hearkened to the voice of Sarai [Gen. 16:2].

The thing that Sarai has suggested was the common practice of that day. When a wife couldn't bear a child, there was the concubine to bear a child. That was according to the law and the custom of that day. However, this does not mean that God approved of it. God did not approve of it at all, and He will make that quite evident. They had been brought up in Ur of the Chaldees in which this was a common practice.

The moral problem is not the thing which is brought out as being so terrible. They committed a sin, and it *was* sin, and God treated it as such. It was sin for Abram to take Hagar, Sarah's maid. But the thing that is pointed out as being so terrible is the cause behind it and that is their unbelief. So often today we reverse this. We make a big issue about some sin but we don't pay too much attention to the unbelief. Unbelief is the real root sin here. It is blacker than all the others.

This suggestion to do according to the custom of that day came from Sarah. It looks as if Abraham has surrendered his position as head of the home here, as we find him following her suggestion.

> And Sarai Abram's wife took Hagar her maid the Egyptian, after Abram had dwelt ten years in the land of Canaan, and gave her to her husband Abram to be his wife.

> And he went in unto Hagar, and she conceived: and when she saw that she had conceived, her mistress was despised in her eyes.

> And Sarai said unto Abram, My wrong be upon thee: I have given my maid into thy bosom; and when she saw that she had conceived, I was despised in her eyes: the LORD judge between me and thee [Gen. 16:3-5].

This little Egyptian maid becomes a concubine and this is not according to God's will. God is not going to accept the offspring from this because it is wrong. God did not approve of this. It is in the record of Scriptures because it is an historical fact that took place, but this does not mean that God approved it.

We can see the problems arising. Hagar despised Sarah because she could mother a child for Abraham which Sarah could not do. So she looked down on Sarah. Then Sarah realizes that she has done wrong. "My wrong be upon thee." She was in the wrong, my friend. God will not accept this, and it is going to be a real heartbreak to old Abraham. They were not really trusting God as they should have. After all, Abraham at this time is 90 years old and Sarah is 80. I think they have come to the conclusion that they are not going to have a child.

I'm sure Sarah could rationalize and think that maybe this is the way God wanted her to act — that they should go by the custom of the day. Yet, it was contrary to God's way of doing things. Remember, friend, just because something is in the Bible does not mean that God approves it. This Book is inspired as

CHAPTER XVI

being an accurate record. There are many things of which God
did not approve which are recorded in His Word. This happens to
be one of them.

HAGAR FLEES FROM SARAI BUT THE ANGEL OF THE LORD BADE HER RETURN

> But Abram said unto Sarai, Behold, thy maid is in thy
> hand; do to her as it pleaseth thee. And when Sarai dealt
> hardly with her, she fled from her face [Gen. 16:6].

Hagar took off. She ran away. It would probably have meant
death to her and certainly death to the child. So the Angel of the
Lord came to her. I am inclined to believe that He is none other
than the pre-incarnate Christ, and that this is characteristic of
Him. He is always out looking for the lost.

> And the angel of the LORD found her by a fountain of
> water in the wilderness, by the fountain in the way to
> Shur.
>
> And he said, Hagar, Sarai's maid, whence camest thou?
> and whither wilt thou go? And she said, I flee from the
> face of my mistress Sarai.
>
> And the angel of the LORD said unto her, Return to thy
> mistress, and submit thyself under her hands.
>
> And the angel of the LORD said unto her, I will multiply
> thy seed exceedingly, that it shall not be numbered for
> multitude [Gen. 16:7-10].

She had gotten quite a distance from home before the angel of
the Lord appeared to her. Paul, in the fourth chapter of the
Epistle to the Galatians, uses this whole incident as an allegory,
and he explains the meaning to us. He speaks of Hagar and her
offspring as representing Mount Sinai where the Mosaic Law was
given. There is a legality of it and there is a bondage of it. Then
he speaks of Sarah, the one who is free. The one who actually
belonged to Abraham was Sarah who was his wife. Now, my
friend, we as believers have been joined to Christ. The church
has been espoused to Christ, Paul says, as a chaste virgin, which
will some day become the bride of Christ. Now as a believer you

do not want to put yourself under the Mosaic Law. You and I don't need that. That would be like Hagar, and that is the point Paul is making in Galatians. If you are the bride of Christ, if you are free like Sarah, then don't try to be like Hagar by putting yourself under the Law.

You see, this whole affair is going to be a great sorrow. It is that already for Sarah, but it won't affect her alone. It is going to be a greater sorrow even to Abraham later on.

Now the angel of the Lord talks about the boy. That boy happens to be Abraham's son.

> **And the angel of the LORD said unto her, Behold, thou art with child, and shalt bear a son, and shalt call his name Ishmael; because the LORD hath heard thy affliction.**
>
> **And he will be a wild man; his hand will be against every man, and every man's hand against him; and he shall dwell in the presence of all his brethren [Gen. 16:11, 12].**

Have you looked at this verse in the light of about 4,000 years of history? Have you looked at the Middle East and what is going on out there today? He's a "wild man" — that has been the story of those Bedouin tribes of the desert down through the centuries. These are the offspring of Ishmael and it is a fulfillment of the prophecy that God gave. They will tell you out there that they are the sons of Ishmael. They are also the sons of Abraham, but they go back to Abraham through Ishmael.

> **And she called the name of the LORD that spake unto her, Thou God seest me: for she said, Have I also here looked after him that seeth me?**
>
> **Wherefore the well was called Beer-lahai-roi; behold, it is between Kadesh and Bered [Gen. 16:13, 14].**

God is gracious to her. It is not *her* sin; so God very graciously deals with her. And I firmly believe that the angel of the Lord here is none other than the pre-incarnate Christ gone out to seek the lost. He is that kind of a Shepherd.

She now had a new concept of God. She realized that He saw her and that was something new to her. She probably had a very primitive idea of God. She is overwhelmed by the fact that she is seen by God.

That doesn't seem to be very impressive to us today because we have a higher view of God than that. But, wait a minute, we probably come just as far short of really knowing about God as she does. It is difficult for a little, finite man to conceive of the infinite God. We all come short of understanding and of knowing Him. I think that is a theme that will engage us throughout the endless ages of eternity, just coming to know God. That is worthy of any man's study. Learning to know God is something that will dignify man's position throughout eternity.

BIRTH OF ISHMAEL

And Hagar bare Abram a son: and Abram called his son's name, which Hagar bare, Ishmael.

And Abram was fourscore and six years old, when Hagar bare Ishmael to Abram [Gen. 16:15, 16].

Remember that Ishmael is Abraham's son. Abraham is now eighty-six years old.

Before we go on into the next chapter, I'd like to recapitulate what we have previously said about God testing Abraham. God appeared to him seven times. We have noted that there were certain failures in the life of Abraham, but there were also successes. I'd like to outline the seven tests which God gave to Abraham.

1. God called him out of Ur of the Chaldees to leave his native land, his home town, and his relatives. He was to give up personal ambitions and plans. Abraham responded to this partially. His faith was weak and imperfect but at least he did move out. The final result was that he arrived in the land of Canaan safely, blessed of God.

2. There was a famine in the land of Canaan. Abram fled from the land of Canaan and went down to Egypt. There he acquired riches and Hagar, about whom we have just been talking. Both were a stumbling block to him.

3. Abraham was given riches and they are a real test. They have been a stumbling block to many a man, by the way. Frankly, I've always wished the Lord would have let me have that kind of a test rather than some of the others that I've had. But I am of the opinion He couldn't have trusted me with riches. Abraham actually did not forget God. He was certainly generous and magnanimous toward his nephew Lot, but riches did separate him from Lot. Then God appeared to him again.

4. Abraham was given power by the defeat of the kings of the East. That was a real test, since he was the conqueror. Then Melchizedek met him, and I think that strengthened Abraham for the test; so he refused the spoils of war. Again God appeared to Abraham and encouraged him.

5. God delayed giving Abraham a son by his wife Sarah. They both became impatient and through the prompting of Sarah, he took matters into his own hands and moved outside the will of God. This resulted in the birth of Ishmael. The Arabs of the desert today still plague the nation Israel, and they will keep right on doing it, I think, until the Millennium.

6. We will see later that the sixth test was the destruction of Sodom and Gomorrah. Abraham thought there were many righteous people in the cities; so he interceded for these cities. From this, Abraham discovered that the Judge of the earth does right. God does not destroy the righteous with the wicked.

7. The offering of Isaac. In this he obeyed God implicitly and completely. Abraham has now arrived at the place where he is the man of faith that God wanted him to be.

CHAPTER 17

This chapter is the key to the book of Genesis. Some feel that it is the key chapter of the Bible. In it God makes His covenant with Abraham and changes the name of Abram to Abraham. Also, God confirms His promise to Abraham about a son.

God's covenant with Abraham concerns two important items here. This concerns a seed and a land. God reveals Himself to Abraham by a new name, *El Shaddai*, the Almighty God. Also, He gives Abraham a new name. I've been using both names, calling him Abram and Abraham, but actually up to this point his name was Abram and now it is changed to Abraham. Abram means "high father" and Abraham means "father of a multitude." Ishmael is not the son whom God promised Abraham even though God does promise to make a great nation of him. This chapter makes it clear that there is to be another son.

GOD APPEARS TO ABRAHAM BY A NEW NAME (ALMIGHTY GOD) AND HE GIVES ABRAM A NEW NAME (ABRAHAM)

We will find now that Abraham is ninety-nine years old. He was eighty-six years old when Ishmael was born, and it was not until about fourteen years later that Isaac was born.

And when Abram was ninety years old and nine, the LORD appeared to Abram, and said unto him, I am the Almighty God; walk before me, and be thou perfect [Gen. 17:1].

God reveals to Abraham a new name, El Shaddai, the Almighty God.

And I will make my covenant between me and thee, and will multiply thee exceedingly [Gen. 17:2].

This word *covenant* appears in this chapter thirteen times. There are twenty-seven verses in the chapter; so when *covenant* appears thirteen times, you know it is very important. Obviously, God is talking about the covenant. Let us listen to Him.

"I will make my covenant between Me and thee, and will multiply thee exceedingly."

This is God's fifth appearance to Abraham. Not only is it another appearance to this man, but now He comes to make the covenant and to reaffirm the promise that He has made about a son. This absolutely rules out the boy, Ishmael, as being the promised son, which I'm sure is one of the important reasons it occurred at this point.

Paul talks about this in the fourth chapter of Romans.

> And being not weak in faith, he considered not his own body now dead, when he was about an hundred years old, neither yet the deadness of Sarah's womb [Rom. 4:19].

Sarah's womb actually was a tomb, a place of death. Out of death came life — Isaac was born. Now Paul concludes the chapter by making a likeness between Isaac being born out of a dead womb and the resurrection of Jesus our Lord.

> Who was delivered for our offences, and was raised again for our justification [Rom. 4:25].

Life out of death. That is exactly the promise that God is making to Abraham. He is ninety-nine years old and that means Sarah is eighty-nine years old. When Isaac was born, Abraham was one hundred years old and Sarah was ninety.

And Abram fell on his face: and God talked with him, saying, As for me, behold, my covenant is with thee, and thou shalt be a father of many nations [Gen. 17:3, 4].

You will be the father of many nations. Just think of it! For about 4,000 years there have been the two great lines from Abraham. There is the line of Ishmael and the line of Isaac, and there have been millions in each line. What a family! Then add to that the spiritual seed of Abraham, we who are called the children of God by faith in Christ. That is the reason Paul, in Romans 4:16, calls Abraham the father of us all. He is the father of the believers in Christ, of the nation Israel, and of the Arabs. Certainly God made good his promise. He said over 4,000 years ago that Abraham would be the father of many nations.

Neither shall thy name any more be called Abram, but thy name shall be Abraham; for a father of many nations have I made thee [Gen. 17:5].

Abram means "high father" or "father of the height." We would say "exalted father." And *Abraham* means father of a multitude.

Now let's inject a little story here to illustrate something of the faith of this man Abraham. Suppose one morning that Abraham and Sarah got up and were working around the tent, and some traders came from the desert. They would stop at their little oasis there at the spring at Hebron and get water from the well as they traveled from the north on their way down to Egypt. They would ask for water for themselves and their camels, and Abraham would go out to meet them. We must remember that there were a great many hospitable people in that day. It's quite interesting that we speak of primitive man way back yonder as being terrible, yet in that day a stranger couldn't go through the country without somebody opening his home to him and entertaining him. But if you came into Los Angeles as a stranger I don't know anybody who would take you in although there are a lot of Christians in that area. Our culture is altogether different. We certainly lack the hospitality they had in that day.

Abraham would go out to meet them and tell them to help themselves to water and he'd feed their stock. Then he'd say, "Are you staying for a while?" They would answer, "No, we're in a hurry to get down to Egypt." They would introduce themselves and one man would be Allah and another would be Ali Baba; then they'd ask Abraham what his name was. He would answer, "My name is High Father." So they would say, "Well, is it a boy or a girl?" and Abraham would tell them he didn't have any children. Don't you see how they would laugh? "You mean to tell us that you don't have any children and your name is Abram?" So they would ride off into the desert, laughing.

Then six months later they would come back on their return trip and would stop again and Abraham would go out to meet them. They would begin to laugh and say, "Hello, High Father." Then Abraham would tell them, "My name is not High Father anymore." So they would ask him what his new name was. He would answer, "Father of a multitude." Then they would be curious and say, "My! must have been twins!" Abraham would then tell them that he still didn't have any children. Then they would really laugh. How ridiculous can a man be? Here is a man who is a father before he has any children.

Think of the faith of this man Abraham. But 4,000 years later, where you and I sit, we're not laughing. God made him a father of many nations. That name "stuck," if you please, and he is still Abraham, the father of a multitude.

GOD'S COVENANT WITH ABRAHAM ABOUT A SEED AND THE LAND

And I will make thee exceeding fruitful, and I will make nations of thee, and kings shall come out of thee.

And I will establish my covenant between me and thee and thy seed after thee in their generations for an everlasting covenant, to be a God unto thee, and to thy seed after thee.

And I will give unto thee, and to thy seed after thee, the land wherein thou art a stranger, all the land of Canaan, for an everlasting possession; and I will be their God [Gen. 17:6-8].

God has certainly made kings come out of Abraham and has made nations come from him. God makes an everlasting covenant with Abraham. It is everlasting, and that means it is still good today. You see, God has promised you and me everlasting life if we will trust Christ. That is a covenant God has made with us. My friend, if God is not going to make good the one He made to Abraham, then you'd better look into yours again. But I have news for you! He's going to make yours good and He's also going to make Abraham's good.

Notice that God says, "I will . . . I will . . . I will." And the covenant that God will do is an everlasting covenant. It cannot be broken. It is not one that is going to run out. This is not a ninety-nine-year lease that God gave them on the Promised Land. God gave them an everlasting possession.

During the course of history, they have lived on the land during three periods. The land is theirs, but the important thing is that they occupy it only under certain conditions. God first of all sent them down into the land of Egypt, during the days of Joseph, where they became a nation. They went down as a family of about seventy and they came out a nation of a million and a half or more. Then they were put out of the land in the Babylonian captivity because they had gone into idolatry and were not witnessing for God. They were brought back into the land to be dispersed again in A. D. 70 after they had rejected their Messiah. God predicted that they would be put out of the land three times and He said they would be returned three times. They have been returned twice. (I do not consider the present return to the land a fulfillment.) When they return the next time, I understand it means they will never go out of it again. This will happen when the Millennium takes place, when God gathers them and brings them back in the land.

CIRCUMCISION, THE BADGE OF THE COVENANT

And God said unto Abraham, Thou shalt keep my covenant therefore, thou, and thy seed after thee in their generations.

This is my covenant, which ye shall keep, between me and you and thy seed after thee; Every man child among you shall be circumcised [Gen. 17:9, 10].

Circumcision is the badge of the covenant. They didn't go through this rite in order to become a member of the covenant. They did this because they had a covenant from God. That makes all the difference in the world.

It is the same relationship concerning good works for the believer today. The believer does not perform good works in order to get saved. He performs good works because he has been saved. Let me illustrate: When I was a boy and when I went away from home, I got into a lot of trouble. The one thing that kept me from becoming an absolute renegade was my Dad. I said, "Because I'm the son of my father, I won't do this and I won't enter into that." I refrained because of him. Now, I didn't become his son because I didn't do certain things. I was already his son. It was because I was his son that I didn't do certain things.

It was not the circumcision which put them under the covenant. It was the evidence of it, the badge of it.

And he that is eight days old shall be circumcised among you ... [Gen. 17:12].

Have you noticed how meticulously all is recorded concerning the birth of Christ? All the law was fulfilled in connection with the birth of this little Baby. He was the son of Abraham and He was the son of David. Since He was in that line, on the eighth day He was circumcised. Paul tells us that Christ was born under the law.

He that is born in thy house, and he that is bought with thy money, must needs be circumcised: and my covenant shall be in your flesh for an everlasting covenant [Gen. 17:13].

They didn't do the circumcising in order to get the covenant. God had already made it for them. I trust that you see this. It is so important for you to see it because the same thing is true today.

You see, a great many people think that if they join the church or if they get baptized, then they will be saved. No, my friend, these things do not save you. If you are saved, I do think that you would do both of those things. I think you would join a church and I think you would be baptized. But you don't do that to get saved. We need to keep the cart where it belongs, following the horse, and not get the cart before the horse. In fact, in the thinking of many people they actually have the horse in the cart!

And the uncircumcised man child whose flesh of his foreskin is not circumcised, that soul shall be cut off from his people; he hath broken my covenant [Gen. 17:14].

There were those in Israel who disobeyed the command to be circumcised. We will find out that practically the entire nation disobeyed this when they came out of the land of Egypt. This did not militate against the covenant. It did mean that the individual would be put out. No individual or group could destroy this covenant with the nation. God had made this with Abraham and with his seed after him, and it is an everlasting covenant.

When man has broken the covenant, the man is put out, but the covenant stands. How marvelous!

GOD CHANGES SARAI'S NAME TO SARAH AND PROMISES SHE SHALL HAVE A SON

And God said unto Abraham, As for Sarai thy wife, thou shalt not call her name Sarai, but Sarah shall her name be.

And I will bless her, and give thee a son also of her: yea, I will bless her, and she shall be a mother of nations; kings of people shall be of her [Gen. 17:15, 16].

Although I've been calling her Sarah all along, it truly was *Sarai* before and now it is changed to *Sarah*. And if old Abraham is going to be a father of nations, then Sarah is going to be a mother of nations.

Then Abraham fell upon his face, and laughed, and said in his heart, Shall a child be born unto him that is an hundred years old? and shall Sarah, that is ninety years old, bear? [Gen. 17:17].

Old Abraham — he just laughed! Now it's not the laughter of unbelief. I think it is the laughter of sheer joy. You know, every now and then in our lives God does something for us that is just so wonderful. I'm sure you have had such an experience that you don't know anything else to do but just to laugh about it. Put yourself back in his position and you'll realize that this was something unheard of. There was the deadness of Sarah's womb, and in effect, Abraham was dead. Paul writes about this:

(As it is written, I have made thee a father of many nations,) before him whom he believed, even God, who quickeneth the dead, and calleth those things which be not as though they were.

Who against hope believed in hope, that he might become the father of many nations; according to that which was spoken, So shall thy seed be.

And being not weak in faith, he considered not his own body now dead, when he was about an hundred years old, neither yet the deadness of Sarah's womb:

He staggered not at the promise of God through unbelief; but was strong in faith, giving glory to God;

And being fully persuaded that, what he had promised, he was able also to perform.

And therefore it was imputed to him for righteousness [Romans 4:17-22].

You see, Abraham believed God, and he is absolutely overwhelmed by the wonder and the goodness of God. But then, all of a sudden, a thought comes to him and it's like an arrow to his heart. You know what? He thinks of a little boy and that little boy is Ishmael.

And Abraham said unto God, O that Ishmael might live before thee!

And God said, Sarah thy wife shall bear thee a son indeed; and thou shalt call his name Isaac: and I will establish my covenant with him for an everlasting covenant, and with his seed after him [Gen. 17:18, 19].

Abraham is saying now, "Oh Lord, this little fellow that has been growing up in my home . . ." You see, he's attached to him. Ishmael was fourteen years old when Abraham sent him out and I don't think Abraham ever saw him again. It broke his heart to send the boy away. After all, friend, regardless of what you might think of Ishmael, he was Abraham's son. Abraham loved this son and it was a heartbreak for him to have to give him up. I'm of the opinion that he must have thought many, many times, "I made a great big mistake in taking Hagar." That was his sin. It plagued not only him, friend, but look over in that land today. There's been trouble in that land from the beginning. Why? Because Abraham sinned.

Don't try to tell me sin is a little thing. Or don't say that sin is something you get by with.

Be not deceived; God is not mocked: for whatsoever a man soweth, that shall he also reap [Gal. 6:7].

There are the fruits of sin. One doesn't just reap something similar but just "that." This man Abraham is reaping now. "Oh, that Ishmael might live before thee!"

God tells him that Sarah shall have a son. He is saying in effect that Ishmael is not the son of promise. What Abraham did was wrong. Don't ever say that God approved polygamy. He is condemning it right here. He does not give his approval to the act of Abraham.

ISHMAEL ALSO TO BECOME A GREAT NATION

And as for Ishmael, I have heard thee: Behold, I have blessed him, and will make him fruitful, and will multiply him exceedingly; twelve princes shall he beget, and I will make him a great nation.

But my covenant will I establish with Isaac, which Sarah shall bear unto thee at this set time in the next year.

And he left off talking with him, and God went up from Abraham [Gen. 17:20-22].

God holds to the promise that He has made. He is not to be deterred or deferred from it at all. He is going to do the exact thing that He said He would do. He speaks as if Isaac is already born and already in their midst. He speaks of things that are not as if they are. Isaac will not be born until the next year.

The Lord stops talking to Abraham. It is as if He is saying, "Abraham, you might as well keep quiet." God has already decided. Friend, there are times when we should stop petitioning the Lord. There are certain things we don't need to ask Him. There are times when we have said enough and don't need to say any more. I'm of the opinion that a great many folk just pester the Lord in a prayer and they already have the answer which is no. Abraham should not mention Ishmael anymore. Isaac is to be the son of the inheritance and God will not change that.

This does not mean that God is not going to listen to Abraham's prayers. We will find a little later that God did listen to Abraham, but it was not about this matter. I sometimes find people praying about things that God doesn't intend to answer. Remember that we are taught to pray in the will of God. I try to be careful when I ask people to pray about certain things. We should pray for those things which are reasonable for God to answer.

And Abraham took Ishmael his son, and all that were born in his house, and all that were bought with his money, every male among the men of Abraham's house; and circumcised the flesh of their foreskin in the self-same day, as God had said unto him [Gen. 17:23].

This is the badge of the covenant that God had made with Abraham. The question will rise as to why Ishmael was included in the rite of circumcision. It is because God had promised that he would be a great nation also. He is included in the covenant in that sense, but he is not to be the one whom God had promised to Abraham in the beginning. He is not to be the father of that nation which God will use and from whom the Messiah will come. That is very important for us to see. The Messiah will come through Isaac.

And Abraham was ninety years old and nine, when he was circumcised in the flesh of his foreskin.

And Ishmael his son was thirteen years old, when he was circumcised in the flesh of his foreskin.

In the selfsame day was Abraham circumcised, and Ishmael his son.

And all the men of his house, born in the house, and bought with money of the stranger, were circumcised with him [Gen. 17:24-27].

CHAPTER 18

This is the chapter about the destruction of Sodom and Gomorrah. It is a little more lengthy chapter, and we are going to hit some of the high points. In chapter 18, Abraham is told about the judgment upon these cities by God and he intercedes with God for them. We could call this a chapter about the "blessed life." It shows the blessed Christian life in fellowship with God.

The story is continued on into chapter 19 where the actual destruction is related. Lot made the decision to live there and must escape from the doomed cities. I guess we could call that the "blasted life." What a difference! All because of a decision that Lot made!

The blessed Christian life is a life in fellowship with God. God then reveals His Person and His plans to Abraham, and Abraham could act as an intercessor on behalf of others. That is the sweet portion of every child of God who stays in the will of God.

Lot is an example of the blasted Christian life. Unfortunately, we have both kinds among Christians today. There are those today who have made real shipwreck of their lives. They have gotten out of the will of God. I wouldn't suggest for a moment that they have lost their salvation, but they certainly have lost everything else. As Paul says, they are saved yet so as by fire.

GOD APPEARS TO ABRAHAM ON PLAINS OF MAMRE AND REAFFIRMS HIS PROMISE TO GIVE ABRAHAM A SON

And the LORD appeared unto him in the plains of Mamre: and he sat in the tent door in the heat of the day;

And he lift up his eyes and looked, and, lo, three men stood by him: and when he saw them, he ran to meet them from the tent door, and bowed himself toward the ground [Gen. 18:1, 2].

Abraham is an old man. Notice how hospitable Abraham is. The little story I told you last time does have a basis in fact, you see, although I don't think it ever literally took place.

And said, My Lord, if now I have found favour in thy sight, pass not away, I pray thee, from thy servant:

Let a little water, I pray you, be fetched, and wash your feet, and rest yourselves under the tree [Gen. 18:3, 4].

We would find it very strange to tell a stranger who comes to see us to wash his feet and come in. We wouldn't quite say that today. Yet, this is probably the oldest custom that is known. Remember that in the Upper Room our Lord washed the disciples' feet. That had a tremendous spiritual message. Here, Abraham is washing their feet as a token of real hospitality. In that day they didn't take off their hat when they came into the house; they took off their shoes. Today we have reversed that so we leave our shoes on and take off our hat. I would prefer it their way. I like to go barefoot in the summertime and I wish it were possible. When I'm out in Hawaii, I put away my shoes and wear thongs or go barefoot. I think this was a great custom. I'm sure it made you feel at home to take off your shoes, wash your feet, and rest yourself under the tree.

And I will fetch a morsel of bread, and comfort ye your hearts; after that ye shall pass on: for therefore are ye come to your servant. And they said, So do, as thou hast said.

And Abraham hastened into the tent unto Sarah, and said, Make ready quickly three measures of fine meal, knead it, and make cakes upon the hearth.

And Abraham ran unto the herd, and fetcht a calf tender and good, and gave it unto a young man; and he hasted to dress it.

And he took butter, and milk, and the calf which he had dressed, and set it before them; and he stood by them under the tree and they did eat [Gen. 18:5-8].

Abraham entertains royally and prepares a bounteous meal. They had veal steaks or veal roast with all the trimmings.

Abraham didn't know who he was actually entertaining. All he knew was that he had three guests. This incident is mentioned in the New Testament where we are urged to be hospitable.

> Be not forgetful to entertain strangers: for thereby some have entertained angels unawares [Heb. 13:2].

> **And they said unto him, Where is Sarah thy wife? And he said, Behold, in the tent.**

> **And he said, I will certainly return unto thee according to the time of life, and, lo, Sarah thy wife shall have a son. And Sarah heard it in the tent door, which was behind him [Gen. 18:9, 10].**

In that day, it wasn't proper for the wife to come out and be the one to entertain guests. This was especially true if the guests were male guests. As you know, this is still true in the East today. So the guests asked about Sarah. Sarah had her ear to the keyhole as she had been listening in. Now both Abraham and Sarah realize that they are entertaining angels unaware.

> **Now Abraham and Sarah were old and well stricken in age; and it ceased to be with Sarah after the manner of women.**

> **Therefore Sarah laughed within herself, saying, After I am waxed old shall I have pleasure, my lord being old also? [Gen. 18:11, 12].**

She laughs at the possibility of her having a son. Now what kind of laughter is this? Well, I think this is the laughter that says it is just too good to be true. May I remind you again that I'm sure most of us have had experiences like that. God has been so good to us and on a certain occasion we just laughed as Abraham did. Something happened that was just too good to be true. That was the way Sarah laughed. However, it frightened her because God spoke to Abraham about it.

> **And the LORD said unto Abraham, Wherefore did Sarah laugh, saying, Shall I of a surety bear a child, which am old?**

Is any thing too hard for the LORD? At the time appointed I will return unto thee, according to the time of life, and Sarah shall have a son.

Then Sarah denied, saying, I laughed not; for she was afraid. And he said, Nay; but thou didst laugh [Gen. 18:13-15].

She is frightened and she tries to be evasive, but she couldn't avoid the truth.

And the men rose up from thence, and looked toward Sodom: and Abraham went with them to bring them on the way [Gen. 18:16].

Abraham didn't have a front gate; so he walked out with them a little farther than the front gate to bid them goodbye. Abraham lived in a place where, as they walked out, they could look down to Sodom and Gomorrah. When we were in that land, I noticed how far we could see on a clear day. From Jerusalem we could see Bethlehem, and from the ruins of old Samaria we could see Jerusalem. You can see the Mediterranean Sea and the Sea of Galilee, and you can see Mt. Hermon from most anyplace. It is tremendous. Now here, Abraham walks out a ways with these guests, and they can easily see Sodom and Gomorrah down below there. These were great resorts of that day, and must have been very delightful and very beautiful places.

GOD ANNOUNCES THE COMING DESTRUCTION OF SODOM AND GOMORRAH TO ABRAHAM

And the LORD said, Shall I hide from Abraham that thing which I do;

Seeing that Abraham shall surely become a great and mighty nation, and all the nations of the earth shall be blessed in him [Gen. 18:17, 18]?

God knows that He is going to destroy Sodom and Gomorrah, but up to this point that fact has been hidden. Notice the reason that God gives to explain why He is not going to hide it from Abraham. Abraham is going to have a tremendous influence. He is going to influence multitudes of people on into succeeding generations. That's true right here today — we are reading about

Abraham, and he is influencing all of us. We can't avoid it. So God says that He had better not hide this from Abraham or else Abraham will get the wrong impression about God.

> **For I know him, that he will command his children and his household after him, and they shall keep the way of the LORD, to do justice and judgment; that the LORD may bring upon Abraham that which he hath spoken of him.**
>
> **And the LORD said, Because the cry of Sodom and Gomorrah is great, and because their sin is very grievous;**
>
> **I will go down now, and see whether they have done altogether according to the cry of it, which is come unto me; and if not, I will know.**
>
> **And the men turned their faces from thence, and went toward Sodom: but Abraham stood yet before the LORD [Gen. 18:19-22].**

God is telling Abraham that He knows the situation there but that He is going down to investigate. In other words, God never does anything hurriedly or hastily. It is a good thing God told Abraham. If God would have destroyed the cities, Abraham might not have understood and would have thought that God is dictatorial and vindictive. Abraham might have felt that He did not show mercy at all nor show any consideration for those who are His. Then Abraham would have had a really distorted and warped view of God.

God did let Abraham know what He was planning to do. This gave Abraham time to turn it over in his mind. We will see that Abraham did have a wrong idea of God and of Sodom and Gomorrah. He was wrong about many things. This is the reason that God tells us as much as He does. There are a lot of things He doesn't tell us because we do not need to know them. But God does tell us enough of His plans for us to trust in Him.

The two men left to go to Sodom. Abraham stood yet before the Lord.

ABRAHAM APPROACHES GOD AS INTERCESSOR ON BEHALF OF
THE INHABITANTS

> **And Abraham drew near, and said, Wilt thou also
> destroy the righteous with the wicked [Gen. 18:23]?**

You see, this was the first thing that entered his mind. Will
God be fair? Of course, he was thinking of Lot. He had rescued
him once, and now he is in danger again. He's wondering, and
I'm sure had many times wondered about Lot and his
relationship to God. He believes that Lot is a saved man, and so
he asks God what He is going to do about the righteous. I think
Abraham would have told you that there were many people in
Sodom whom he thought were saved people. He couldn't understand God wanting to destroy, and actually going through with
the destruction of the righteous with the wicked. What a picture
we have here!

> **Peradventure there be fifty righteous within the city: wilt
> thou also destroy and not spare the place for the fifty
> righteous that are therein?**

> **That be far from thee to do after this manner, to slay the
> righteous with the wicked: and that the righteous should
> be as the wicked, that be far from thee: Shall not the
> Judge of all the earth do right [Gen. 18:24, 25]?**

Abraham begins with fifty. He is sure the Lord would not
destroy the city if there were fifty righteous people in it. Would
He? Abraham asks the question which has been repeated by
people down through the ages. "Shall not the Judge of all the
earth do right?" There is an answer to that question. The entire
rest of the Bible testifies to the fact that the Judge of all the earth
always does right. Whatever God does is right. If you don't think
He is right, the trouble is not with God but with you and your
thinking. You don't know all the facts; you cannot have all the
details. If you did, you would know that the Judge of all the earth
does right. Our judgment is faulty and limited. He is right.

> **And the LORD said, If I find in Sodom fifty righteous
> within the city, then I will spare all the place for their
> sakes.**

And Abraham answered and said, Behold now, I have taken upon me to speak unto the Lord, which am but dust and ashes:

Peradventure there shall lack five of the fifty righteous: wilt thou destroy all the city for lack of five? And he said, If I find there forty and five, I will not destroy it [Gen. 18:26-28].

Abraham thought over the Lord's first answer and then had the courage to ask Him to spare the city for forty-five believers. When God says He would do this, Abraham becomes more bold. He asks for God to save the city if there are forty righteous men. God tells him He would save the city for forty men. So Abraham keeps on asking. Would God save it for thirty? Yes, He would. Would God save it for twenty? Yes, He would. Abraham is really overwhelmed by now and he takes another real plunge. Would God save the city for ten men? Yes, God would save it for ten righteous men.

And the LORD went his way, as soon as he had left communing with Abraham: and Abraham returned unto his place [Gen. 18:33].

The question we would ask here is why Abraham didn't come down to a number below ten. I'll tell you why. At this point he is afraid that Lot is lost, and this disturbs him a great deal; so he is not going to come down any further. But he could have come down to *one*, friend. He could have said, "Lord, if there is one in that city who is righteous, would you destroy the city?" Do you know what God would have said? He would have told Abraham that He would take that one out of the city because He would not destroy that city with one righteous man in it. How do I know that would have been His answer? Because that is what He did. There was one righteous man there. Abraham thought that Lot was lost but God knew him. God told Lot to get out of that city, because God couldn't destroy it as long as Lot was there.

Do you know that the Tribulation, the Great Tribulation period, can't come as long as true believers are in the world? It just can't come, friend. Christ bore our judgment and the Great Tribulation is part of the judgment that is coming. That is the reason the body of the true believers, which we call the church,

cannot go through it. This is a glorious picture of that truth.
Sodom and Gomorrah are a picture of the world, and what a picture that is! We don't know when the Lord is coming to take us
out of this world. It could be today or tomorrow, but it will be the
same situation as is pictured for us here in Sodom and
Gomorrah.

This concludes a chapter which has given us an insight into
blessed fellowship with God. Now the picture is going to change.
We will leave Hebron up on the plains of Mamre where Abraham
lived, and we will go down to the city of Sodom where Lot lives.

CHAPTER 19

What a change this chapter is from the preceding one. Here we see the "blasted" Christian life. Angels visit with Lot and warn him to escape. He leaves Sodom with his wife and daughters, and then the cities are destroyed. Then the chapter tells us of Lot's awful sin.

TWO ANGELS ARRIVE IN SODOM AND VISIT LOT

And there came two angels to Sodom at even; and Lot sat in the gate of Sodom: and Lot seeing them rose up to meet them; and he bowed himself with his face toward the ground;

And he said, Behold now, my lords, turn in, I pray you, into your servant's house, and tarry all night, and wash your feet, and ye shall rise up early, and go on your ways. And they said, Nay; but we will abide in the street all night.

And he pressed upon them greatly; and they turned in unto him, and entered into his house; and he made them a feast, and did bake unleavened bread, and they did eat [Gen. 19:1-3].

Don't forget that this man Lot is a righteous man. It's hard to believe it. If I had this record alone, I wouldn't believe it, but Simon Peter tells us about Lot in his Epistle.

And delivered just Lot, vexed with the filthy conversation of the wicked.

(For that righteous man dwelling among them, in seeing and hearing, vexed his righteous soul from day to day with their unlawful deeds;) [II Peter 2:7, 8].

He lived in Sodom but he was never happy there. You see, it was really a very tragic day for Lot when he moved to Sodom. Lot lost all that he had and he lost his family — the fact of the matter is, when you look at the total picture, you see he lost all of them. It is really tragic.

There are many men today who may be saved men, but by their lives — where they go, and where and how they live — they lose their family. Such a man loses his influence and loses his testimony. I know Christians like that. I've been a pastor now for quite a few years, and in the course of time I have talked to children of some of the leaders of churches I have served. Not too long ago, such a son of a church leader told me that he was just waiting for his dad to die before he repudiates everything. He thought the whole thing was phony and that all he could see in the Christian life was a lot of hypocrisy. What he was doing, of course, was revealing his home. What a phony his dad must be! And he has lost his son! He has also lost his influence in other places, I can assure you. Yet, I truly believe this man is a Christian who truly trusts Christ.

Poor Lot. That is the way he was!

These men must have had dirty feet after walking from the plains of Mamre down into Sodom with nothing but sandals on their feet. But again, I call your attention to the custom of that day which was practiced by those who extended hospitality to strangers.

Notice that Lot was sitting in the *gate* of Sodom. The ones who sat in the gate of a city were the judges. This man Lot had not only moved to Sodom, but he had gotten into the politics down there. Here he is a petty judge, sitting in the gate.

He is an hospitable man. When these strangers arrive, he invites them to his home and they come in. He prepares a feast for them. They had one with Abraham; now they are having one with Lot.

But notice their first reluctance to come into his home. They said they could stay out on the street and sleep in the park, as it were. So Lot had to tell them they couldn't do that. Not in Sodom! It would be too dangerous! Their life wouldn't be safe if they did a thing like that.

Many of our cities today ought to change their names to Sodom. It wouldn't be safe for you to sleep on their streets either.

In fact, it is not safe to be walking on the streets at night. Many women who live alone will not come out for church or any program in the evening. They lock their door at dark and do not open that door until the next morning in the daylight. It isn't even safe to walk in many of the neighborhoods during the day. We are in the days of Sodom and Gomorrah again and for practically the same reason.

You see how the men brought out all of this in their conversation with Lot.

THE LOW MORAL CONDITION OF SODOM

But before they lay down, the men of the city, even the men of Sodom, compassed the house round, both old and young, all the people from every quarter:

And they called unto Lot, and said unto him, Where are the men which came in to thee this night? bring them out unto us, that we may know them [Gen. 19:4, 5].

This is a sickening scene. It reveals the degradation of this city of Sodom. The name that has been put on that sin from that day until this day is *sodomy*. At least there was no attempt made, apparently, in the city of Sodom to have a church for this crowd to tell them they were all right in spite of the fact that they practiced this thing! May I say to you, the Word of God is very specific on this and you cannot tone it down. It is an awful sin.

I am sure that when Lot first moved down into the city of Sodom, he did not realize what kind of a city it was. After he had moved in, he found out that perversion was the order of the day. He brought up his children in this atmosphere. You will recall that he had looked down toward Sodom and had pitched his tent toward Sodom. What he saw when he looked down there were the lovely streets and the boulevards and the parks and the public buildings, and the folk on the outside. He did not see what was really there. The sin of this city is so great that God is going to judge it. He is going to destroy the city.

Let us draw a sharp line here. Today there is a tendency toward a gray area in the new attitude towards sin. People don't think sodomy is as black as it was once thought to be. Even the church today has compromised until it is pitiful. Right now the

press in southern California is reporting a church made up of
those who are homosexuals. The pastor of the church is also
homosexual. They all freely admit it. May I say to you, the lesson
of Sodom and Gomorrah is a lesson for this generation. God does
not accept that kind of a church. The idea seems to be that you
can become a child of God and then continue on in sin. God says
that is impossible. You cannot do that. This city of Sodom is an
example. You cannot continue in sin.

What shall we say then? Shall we continue in sin, that
grace may abound?

God forbid. How shall we that are dead to sin, live any
longer therein [Romans 6:1, 2]?

This idea today that you can be a Christian and go on in sin is a
tremendous mistake. That's what they were doing in Sodom and
Gomorrah, and God destroyed those cities. Don't say that this a
primitive view of God. Don't say we have a better view of God
today and now we know that, after all, Jesus received sinners. He
surely did! Jesus does receive sinners! But when He gets through
with the sinner, He has changed him! The harlot that came to
Jesus was changed. She was not a harlot any longer. That is the
thing that happened to others who came to Jesus. The publican
came to Him and he left the seat of custom — he gave up his
crooked life when he came to Jesus.

My friend, if you come to Jesus for forgiveness, you will
change. Sin is still sin. I recognize that I will get letters from
people trying to explain to me that we are living in a new day and
that I need to wake up. Friends, it doesn't matter what this
generation is saying. It just happens to be Sodom and Gomorrah
all over again.

**And Lot went out at the door unto them, and shut the
door after him.**

**And said, I pray you, brethren, do not so wickedly [Gen.
19:6, 7].**

The men of Sodom were outside the door asking that these
guests should be turned out to them. Lot calls this wickedness.
Notice the way he looked at it. He's been down there a long time
and it wasn't the new morality to him. It was just old sin!

> Behold now, I have two daughters which have not known
> man; let me, I pray you, bring them out unto you, and do
> ye to them as is good in your eyes: only unto these men
> do nothing; for therefore came they under the shadow of
> my roof [Gen. 19:8].

When a man entertained a guest in that day, he was responsible for that guest. Here Lot is willing to sacrifice his daughters
to protect his guests!

> And they said, Stand back. And they said again, This one
> fellow came in to sojourn, and he will needs be a judge:
> now will we deal worse with thee, than with them. And
> they pressed sore upon the man, even Lot, and came near
> to break the door.
>
> But the men put forth their hand, and pulled Lot into the
> house to them, and shut to the door.
>
> And they smote the men that were at the door of the
> house with blindness, both small and great: so that they
> wearied themselves to find the door [Gen. 19:9-11].

If they hadn't done this, these men would have destroyed Lot.

THE ANGELS WARN LOT TO LEAVE SODOM AND HE ESCAPES TO ZOAR

> And the men said unto Lot, Hast thou here any besides?
> son in law, and thy sons, and thy daughters, and what-
> soever thou hast in the city, bring them out of this place:
>
> For we will destroy this place, because the cry of them is
> waxen great before the face of the LORD; and the LORD
> hath sent us to destroy it.
>
> And Lot went out, and spake unto his sons in law, which
> married his daughters, and said, Up, get you out of this
> place: for the LORD will destroy this city. But he seemed
> as one that mocked unto his sons in law [Gen. 19:12-14].

Lot is in a very bad situation. He had spent years now down in
the city of Sodom. He had learned to tolerate this sort of thing
although he calls it wickedness. He saw his sons and daughters

grow up, and they, apparently, married among the people of that city. Now, when Lot got this word from the Lord to leave the city, he went to his sons-in-law and he said, "Let's get out of here. God will destroy this city." They just laughed at him and ridiculed him. They probably knew that the week before he had invested a little money in real estate down there. You see, this man was out of the will of God in this place, and so he had no witness for God. He didn't win anybody in this city. Friend, when you go down to the level of the people of the world, you don't win them either. That, I think, is being demonstrated in this hour.

We would think Lot was not saved if we had not learned in II Peter that he was a righteous man and had never really enjoyed it down there. He's going to leave the city, and the only ones he can get to go with him are his wife and his two single daughters.

> **And when the morning arose, then the angels hastened Lot, saying, Arise, take thy wife, and thy two daughters, which are here; lest thou be consumed in the iniquity of the city.**

> **And while he lingered, the men laid hold upon his hand, and upon the hand of his wife, and upon the hand of his two daughters; the LORD being merciful unto him: and they brought him forth, and set him without the city [Gen. 19:15, 16].**

You see, here is God's man. Peter calls him a righteous man. He had become righteous because he had followed Abraham in that he had believed God and had offered the sacrifices to God. Now the Lord God is merciful to him. He really extends His mercy and he gets him out of the city.

> **And it came to pass, when they had brought them forth abroad, that he said, Escape for thy life; look not behind thee, neither stay thou in all the plain; escape to the mountain, lest thou be consumed [Gen. 19:17].**

Even Lot didn't want to leave.

> **And Lot said unto them, Oh, not so, my Lord:**

> **Behold now, thy servant hath found grace in thy sight,**

**and thou hast magnified thy mercy, which thou hast
shewed unto me in saving my life; and I cannot escape to
the mountain, lest some evil take me, and I die:**

**Behold now, this city is near to flee unto, and it is a little
one: Oh, let me escape thither, (is it not a little one?) and
my soul shall live [Gen. 19:18-20].**

He would get out of the city but was afraid he couldn't make it
to the mountain. So he went to a little town named Zoar. You
see, he came out of Sodom, but this man would not make a clean
break with it. So he is still going to get into a great deal of
trouble.

Now God destroyed the city of Sodom. The story goes on to tell
us two things here. One concerns Lot's wife and the other concerns his daughters. His wife looked back from behind him and
she became a pillar of salt. This, I think, has been greatly misunderstood. Why in the world did Mrs. Lot turn and look back? I
think there are two reasons.

She turned and looked back, first of all, because she did not
want to leave Sodom. She loved Sodom. She probably loved Lot,
too, but it was the Lot of Sodom that she loved and she didn't
want to leave. I imagine she was a member of the country club,
the sewing club, and the Shakespeare club. They may have had a
nice little religious club, too. She was right in the thick of it all.
She didn't want to leave. Her body walked out but she surely left
her heart there.

This is a tremendous lesson for us today. I hear a great many
Christians today who talk about wanting to see the Lord come,
but they are not living like it. On Sunday morning it is difficult
to get them to leave their comfortable bed and lovely home. On
Sunday night they aren't going to leave their television — they
don't want to miss the programs; so they would rather not go to
church. Friend, when the Lord comes, we're going to leave the
TV and that lovely home — everything down here. I have a question to ask you. Will it break your heart to leave all of this?

I ask myself that question many times. I'm not anxious to
leave, to be honest with you. I'd love to stay. I have my loved
ones, my home, and my friends, and I want to be with them. I

have a ministry and I want to carry it on. But I also want to be able to say when He does call that I don't have a thing down here that will break my heart to leave. Not a thing! I don't want to turn and look back.

Secondly, she didn't believe God. God had said they should leave the city and not look back. Lot didn't look back because he believed God. But Mrs. Lot didn't believe God would destroy beautiful Sodom. She wasn't a believer and so she didn't really make it out of the city. She turned into a pillar of salt.

I am not going into detail on the two incidents in this chapter. The destruction of the cities of the plain did occur, and then there is the awful sin of Lot with his two daughters. It is as sordid as it can be.

Frankly, Lot didn't do well by moving down to the city of Sodom. He lost everything except his own soul. You know, that is a picture of a great many people today who will not judge the sins in their lives. They are saved but just "so as by fire." The Lord has said in a very definite way that when folks refuse to judge sin in their lives, then God will judge it. Apparently that was the case with Lot.

I do not want to leave this chapter without a look at Abraham.

And Abraham gat up early in the morning to the place where he stood before the LORD:

And he looked toward Sodom and Gomorrah, and toward all the land of the plain, and beheld, and, lo, the smoke of the country went up as the smoke of a furnace [Gen. 19:27, 28].

When Abraham looked down there, I think his heart was anxious, not knowing if Lot had escaped or not, but Abraham hadn't invested a dime down there so that when judgment came, it didn't disturb him one whit. He wasn't in love with the things of Sodom and the things of this world.

It is too bad that the church is not looking at the sin of sodomy as the Lord looks at it. I don't think it is any greater today than it has been in the past. There is a tremendous percentage of our population that is homosexual and that engages in perversion. Today we speak of it in a more candid manner than we ever did. In fact, ten years ago I would probably never have mentioned it like this in print. Now it is something that is discussed all around us. What is to be the attitude of the Christian toward it today? Lot, in his day, knew that it was wickedness. God judged it. Isn't that enough so that the child of God today knows he is not to compromise with this type of thing? It is sin. Some say that to indulge in it is a sickness. The same thing is said about alcoholism. Surely, it is a sickness. Of course, such a person is sick. But what made him take the first drink and then continue to drink until he became sick? Sin did, friend. Sin is the problem. This is a sin, and it is so labelled in the first chapter of Romans. God says there that He gave them up. So this chapter of Genesis is a very important chapter for our present generation today.

CHAPTER 20

Here is a chapter that just seems to be unnecessary, and I'm going to hit only the high points. What we find here is something we would like to leave out. Abraham repeats the sin that he committed when he went down into the land of Egypt concerning Sarah. He lied about her and called her his sister. Now it is the same sordid story again.

One wonders why this chapter is put here. It seems about as necessary as a fifth leg on a cow. Yet it is here for a very important reason, friend. Abraham and Sarah are going to have to deal with this sin before they can have Isaac, before they can have the blessing. May I say to you, until you and I are willing to deal with the sin in our lives, there is no blessing for us. This was a sinful compact that Abraham and Sarah had in every place they went. Instead of trusting God, they entered into this conspiracy which was a half-truth. This had to be judged before they could have a son, and before Abraham could be brought to the final test of offering Isaac.

ABRAHAM GOES TO GERAR AND MISREPRESENTS HIS RELATIONSHIP TO SARAH

And Abraham journeyed from thence toward the south country, and dwelled between Kadesh and Shur, and sojourned in Gerar.

And Abraham said of Sarah his wife, She is my sister: and Abimelech king of Gerar sent, and took Sarah [Gen. 20:1, 2].

This is quite interesting. Do you think Sarah was beautiful? Well, here she is almost ninety years old and she is beautiful! Not many can qualify in this particular department.

Abraham has gone far south in the Land. He is beyond Kadesh-Barnea, where generations later the children of Israel came after their wilderness journey from Egypt, and refused to enter the Promised Land. He has gone down to Gerar (which I do not think he should have done), and he lies about Sarah again.

God then appears to Abimelech, king of Gerar, in a dream. Now I want to read Abraham's confession after Abimelech interviews him. It is the thing that makes this chapter important and reveals the fact that Abraham and Sarah cannot have Isaac until they deal with this sin in their lives. Remember, this sin goes way back to their early agreement.

ABRAHAM ACKNOWLEDGES HIS WRONG

> And Abraham said, Because I thought, Surely the fear of God is not in this place; and they will slay me for my wife's sake.

> And yet indeed she is my sister; she is the daughter of my father, but not the daughter of my mother; and she became my wife [Gen. 20:11, 12].

Abraham is talking to Abimelech who is greatly disturbed that he would lie about his wife. You can see that he is not trusting God. He felt like he was moving down into a godless place but he finds out that Abimelech has a high sense of what is right and wrong. Apparently he was a man who knew God and who put a tremendous value upon character. You will notice that poor Abraham doesn't look good by the side of Abimelech here.

Abraham confesses the whole thing now. It is really a half-truth and a half-lie. She is Abraham's half sister and she is Abraham's wife.

> And it came to pass, when God caused me to wander from my father's house, that I said unto her, This is thy kindness which thou shalt show unto me; at every place whither we shall come, say of me, He is my brother [Gen. 20:13].

We can see here that when they started out, Abraham didn't have complete confidence and trust in God. He and Sarah made a pact that anywhere they went where it looked like Abraham might get killed because of his wife, Sarah would say that he was her brother. That would keep Abraham from being killed, they thought. They had made that little agreement and they had already used it down in Egypt. Now they use it again. That sin must be dealt with before God is going to hear and answer their prayer in sending a son. Isaac will not be born until this is dealt with.

How many Christians today will not judge sin in their lives and so experience no blessing in their lives! I frankly believe that we could have a real revival if many of the believers in our fundamental churches today, and especially those who are in places of leadership, would confess their sins. I do not mean a public confession. I mean that they would deal with the sins that are in their lives. Friends, I don't believe there will be any blessing until sin is dealt with.

> But let a man examine himself, and so let him eat of that bread, and drink of that cup.
>
> For he that eateth and drinketh unworthily, eateth and drinketh damnation to himself, not discerning the Lord's body.
>
> For this cause many are weak and sickly among you, and many sleep.
>
> For if we would judge ourselves, we should not be judged. But when we are judged, we are chastened of the Lord, that we should not be condemned with the world [I Cor. 11:28-32].

Blessing is being withheld today from the church and from the lives of many believers because we won't deal with the sin in our lives.

CHAPTER 21

In the preceding chapter we saw that Abraham and Sarah had to make confession and put away that sin which was a habit with them, and that went back to an agreement they had made twenty-five years previously. Now in this chapter we come to the birth of Isaac, the casting out of Hagar and Ishmael, and Abraham's experience at Beersheba.

THE BIRTH OF ISAAC

> And the LORD visited Sarah as he had said, and the LORD did unto Sarah as he had spoken.

> For Sarah conceived, and bare Abraham a son in his old age, at the set time of which God had spoken to him [Gen. 21:1, 2].

You will notice that there is a very striking similarity between the birth of Isaac and the birth of Christ. I believe that the birth of Isaac is given to us for that very reason. Before Christ came, it set before mankind this great truth. Isaac was born at the set time as God had promised. Christ was born in the fulness of time.

> But when the fulness of the time was come, God sent forth his Son, made of a woman, made under the law [Gal. 4:4].

> And Abraham called the name of his son that was born unto him, whom Sarah bare to him, Isaac.

> And Abraham circumcised his son Isaac being eight days old, as God had commanded him.

> And Abraham was an hundred years old, when his son Isaac was born unto him.

> And Sarah said, God hath made me to laugh, so that all that hear will laugh with me.

And she said, Who would have said unto Abraham, that Sarah should have given children suck? for I have born him a son in his old age.

And the child grew, and was weaned: and Abraham made a great feast the same day that Isaac was weaned [Gen. 21:3-8].

There are some very remarkable truths that we need to lay hold of here. First of all, the birth of Isaac was contrary to nature. Paul in the fourth chapter of Romans, which we have already read, says that Abraham did not count his own body which was "dead" nor yet did he count the "deadness" of Sarah's womb, but had faith in God. God brings forth life out of death. This is a miraculous birth. God did not flash onto the world something new in the supernatural birth of Jesus Christ. He began to prepare man for it. So we find God producing a miraculous birth way back here in the birth of Isaac.

God had to deal with Sarah and with Abraham before Isaac could be born. They had to recognize it would be impossible for them — Abraham was 100 years old and Sarah was 90 years old. In other words, the birth of Isaac must be something that they could not do in themselves.

HAGAR AND ISHMAEL CAST OUT

And Sarah saw the son of Hagar the Egyptian, which she had born unto Abraham, mocking.

Wherefore she said unto Abraham, Cast out this bondwoman and her son: for the son of this bondwoman shall not be heir with my son, even with Isaac [Gen. 21:9, 10].

The coming of this little boy Isaac into that home surely did produce a great deal of difficulty. Ishmael, who is the son of Hagar, is found mocking the new little fellow in the family. Here we begin to see the nature of this boy Ishmael beginning to reveal itself. Up to this point he seems to have been a pretty nice boy, but now the appearance of the new little boy into the family begins to reveal his true colors.

This is an illustration, by the way, of the fact that a believer has two natures. Before you were converted, you had an old nature which controlled you. You did what you wanted to do. "Doing What Comes Naturally" is what the old nature does. What a man does naturally is not always the nicest sort of thing to do, but there is no other nature in him. But when you were born again into the family of God, you received a new nature. When you receive the new nature, a battle begins between the new nature and the old nature.

> For that which I do I allow not: for what I would, that
> do I not; but what I hate, that do I [Rom. 7:15].

Paul is saying that the new nature doesn't want to do what the old nature wants to do, but the old nature is in control. So then, the time comes when a person must make the decision which way he is going to live, which nature is going to rule. You have to make a determination which we call yielding to the Lord. You either permit the Holy Spirit to move in your life and control it, or else you function by the energy of the flesh. There is no third alternative for the child of God.

Here we are told that the son of the bondwoman must be put out. That is true in our life concerning our two natures. It was true in the life of Abraham.

And the thing was very grievous in Abraham's sight because of his son [Gen. 21:11].

After all, as far as the flesh is concerned, Ishmael is his son just as much as Isaac. Isaac has just been born. He is a tiny little baby, and Abraham doesn't know him yet. But his boy Ishmael has been in the home for about fourteen years, and Abraham is very much attached to him. So to send him away is a grievous thing for Abraham to do.

Let me go back again to the thing we said earlier. God did not approve of the procedure that Abraham and Sarah had followed. Now they are reaping the result which is a heartbreak to Abraham. He is going to send this boy away. Sin is sin and God never approves of sin. Although it was a heartbreak to Abraham, God could not accept Ishmael in the place of Isaac, the son of promise.

Poor Sarah just couldn't take it to have that boy around mocking her little boy. Neither can we live with both natures. Each of us must make a decision. "A double minded man is unstable in all his ways" (James 1:8). That explains the instability, the insecurity, among many Christians today. They want to go with the world and yet they want to go with the Lord. They are spiritual schizophrenics. They're trying to do both, which is impossible.

The Greeks had a race where they put two horses together, and a man mounted them with one foot on one horse and the other foot on the other horse. It was a great race as long as the horses stayed together. Similarly you and I have two natures and one is like a black horse and the other a white horse, and these two horses cannot be hitched together. They won't work together. One goes one way, the other goes the opposite way, and you and I have to make up our minds with which we are going — with one nature or the other. That's why we are told:

> Neither yield ye your members as instruments of unrighteousness unto sin: but yield yourselves unto God, as those that are alive from the dead, and your members as instruments of righteousness unto God [Rom. 6:13].

> For what the law could not do, in that it was weak through the flesh, God sending his own Son in the likeness of sinful flesh, and for sin, condemned sin in the flesh:

> That the righteousness of the law might be fulfilled in us, who walk not after the flesh, but after the Spirit [Rom. 8:3, 4].

The law tried to get a hold on man but the old nature couldn't measure up to the requirements of the law. But the Spirit of God can do it. That is the great message that you find here in this.

Then you will notice that the child grew, and when he was weaned, Abraham made a great feast in celebration of that. First, this little fellow lived by feeding on his mother's milk. Then there came a day when he had to be weaned. We are told that we should "As newborn babes, desire the sincere milk of the word, that we may grow thereby" (I Pet. 2:2).There comes a day when you really want to grow up; so you decide that instead of reading your favorite chapters only, you will try to read through the entire Bible. We all need to grow, just as this little boy Isaac needed to be weaned and grow up.

The character of Ishmael, which we see beginning to reveal itself here, is the nature that we see manifested later on in the nation. That nation is antagonistic. His hand is against his brother. That has been characteristic of him down through the centuries.

I have already suggested that there is a comparison between the birth of Isaac and the birth of the Lord Jesus Christ. Actually Isaac's birth is a foreshadowing of the birth of Christ which is set before us. Notice now the similarities:

1. Both had been promised.

You will recall that when God had called Abraham out of Ur of the Chaldees some 25 years earlier, God had promised to him that he should have a son. God promised a son to Abraham and Sarah. Now the 25 years had gone by, and God made good His promise.

God had told the nation Israel that a virgin should conceive and bring forth a son. The day came when He was born in Bethlehem and that was the fulfillment of prophecy. Both of these births had been promised.

2. Both had a long interval between the promise and the fulfillment.

In the case of Isaac, there was a 25-year interval between promise and fulfillment. The promises concerning Christ covered over a thousand years. He was specifically promised to come from the line of David, and David ruled a thousand years before Christ was born. There is quite a remarkable parallel here.

3. The announcement of both births was incredible.

You will recall that before the birth of Isaac, these men who were the "servants of the Lord" visited Abraham on the way to Sodom. They announced that Sarah should have a son which seemed absolutely impossible. And Sarah laughed at the thought.

Let me ask you, who was the first one to raise a question about the virgin birth? Was it some modern theologian? No, it was Mary herself. When the angel made the announcement, she asked how these things could be, seeing she knew not a man. This is indeed another quite striking parallel.

4. Both were named before their birth.

God told Abraham that he should have a son and that he should call his name Isaac (Gen. 17:19). When the angel appeared to Joseph before the birth of our Saviour, the angel told Joseph to name Him Jesus, "for He shall save His people from their sins" (Matt. 1:21).

5. Both births occurred at God's appointed time.

I have already called attention to that in the second verse of this chapter where a son is promised at the set time which God had spoken. We also read in Gal. 4:4 that in the fulness of time God sent forth His Son to be born of a woman.

6. Both births are miraculous.

Abraham was 100 years old and Sarah was 90 years old when Isaac was born. No man had a part in the virgin birth of Christ, and that surely is miraculous.

7. Both sons were a particular joy to their father.

And Abraham called the name of his son that was born unto him, whom Sarah bare to him, Isaac [Gen. 21:3].

This was the name that had been told to Abraham back at the time when God made His announcement to him. Remember that Abraham had laughed because of his sheer joy in having a son.

God, the Father, spoke out of heaven to say, "This is My beloved Son in whom I am well pleased."

8. Both sons were obedient to the father, even unto death.

In the next chapter we will see how Isaac was offered up by his father. He was about 33 years old when this took place, and he was obedient to his father even unto death.

What was true of Isaac was also true of the Lord Jesus Christ. We find in Isaac a wonderful picture of the submission of Christ to the will of the Father.

9. The miraculous birth of Isaac is a picture of the resurrection of Christ.

We have previously quoted Romans 4 where Paul said that Abraham did not count that his own body was dead and that Sarah's womb was dead. Out of death came life. That is a picture of the resurrection, you see. When Paul mentions this, he emphasizes the fact that Christ was delivered because of our offences but that He was raised for our justification. So we have here in Isaac a really quite remarkable picture of the Lord Jesus Christ.

Now as we come back to our chapter, we find that God graciously deals with Abraham and with Hagar and Ishmael.

And God said unto Abraham, Let it not be grievous in thy sight because of the lad, and because of thy bondwoman; in all that Sarah hath said unto thee, hearken unto her voice; for in Isaac shall thy seed be called.

And also of the son of the bondwoman will I make a nation, because he is thy seed.

And Abraham rose up early in the morning, and took bread, and a bottle of water, and gave it unto Hagar, putting it on her shoulder, and the child, and sent her away: and she departed, and wandered in the wilderness of Beer-sheba [Gen. 21:12-14].

God makes it very clear to Abraham that He is not going to accept Ishmael as the one whom He had promised. But He does tell Abraham that He will still carry out His promise that nations shall arise out of Abraham, so that a great nation will come from this boy Ishmael.

> And the water was spent in the bottle, and she cast the child under one of the shrubs.
>
> And she went, and sat her down over against him a good way off, as it were a bowshot: for she said, Let me not see the death of the child. And she sat over against him, and lift up her voice, and wept.
>
> And God heard the voice of the lad; and the angel of God called to Hagar out of heaven, and said unto her, What aileth thee, Hagar? fear not; for God hath heard the voice of the lad where he is.
>
> Arise, lift up the lad, and hold him in thine hand; for I will make him a great nation.
>
> And God opened her eyes, and she saw a well of water; and she went, and filled the bottle with water, and gave the lad drink. And God was with the lad; and he grew, and dwelt in the wilderness, and became an archer.
>
> And he dwelt in the wilderness of Paran: and his mother took him a wife out of the land of Egypt [Gen. 21:15-21].

The Bible is not going to follow the line of Ishmael. He becomes a nation out there in the desert. The Arab is still there today.

ABRAHAM AND ABIMELECH AT BEER-SHEBA

> And it came to pass at that time, that Abimelech and Phichol the chief captain of his host spake unto Abraham, saying, God is with thee in all that thou doest:
>
> Now therefore swear unto me here by God that thou wilt not deal falsely with me, nor with my son, nor with my son's son: but according to the kindness that I have done unto thee, thou shalt do unto me, and to the land wherein thou hast sojourned [Gen. 21:22, 23].

Abimelech wants to make a contract or a treaty with this man Abraham. Abraham and Abimelech became good friends because of this.

Thus they made a covenant at Beer-sheba: then Abimelech rose up, and Phichol the chief captain of his host, and they returned into the land of the Philistines.

And Abraham planted a grove in Beer-sheba, and called there on the name of the LORD, the everlasting God.

And Abraham sojourned in the Philistines' land many days [Gen. 21:32-34].

Notice that Abraham calls upon the name of God everywhere he goes. We are told later on that Abraham was always a stranger and a pilgrim in the land which the Lord God had promised to him. That is very evident at this point.

CHAPTER 22

Candidly it was breathtaking the first time I saw the great truths that depict the cross of Christ in this chapter. As in the birth of Isaac, so also in the sacrifice of Isaac, there is a strange similarity to the sacrifice of our Lord.

James makes a statement in his epistle which I am sure many of us thought was a contradictory statement in the Bible.

> Was not Abraham our father justified by works, when he had offered Isaac his son upon the altar [James 2:21]?

But then Paul says,

> What shall we say then that Abraham our father, as pertaining to the flesh hath found?
>
> For if Abraham were justified by works, he hath whereof to glory; but not before God.
>
> For what saith the scripture? Abraham believed God, and it was counted unto him for righteousness.
>
> Now to him that worketh is the reward not reckoned of grace, but of debt [Romans 4:1-4].

Which one is right? The answer is that they are both right. We need to note that both of them are talking about the same thing. James is not talking about works of the law but he is talking about the works of faith. Paul is talking about justification before God. Paul is quoting from the fifteenth chapter of Genesis when Abraham was just getting under way in a walk of faith. Only God knew his heart. God saw that he believed Him and God counted it to him for righteousness. But then this man failed many times. I'm of the opinion that his neighbors wouldn't see that he was righteous because they would be aware of his failures.

Now the day comes when this man takes his son to be offered on the altar. Even the hard-hearted Philistines would have to say that the works of this man show that he believes what God tells him. So James says that Abraham was justified by works. When? When he offered Isaac. Did Abraham really offer Isaac on the altar? Of course, he didn't. But he was willing to do it. The very act of being willing to offer Isaac is the act that James is talking about. It reveals that he had the works of faith. James is emphasizing the works of faith as displayed here in the twenty-second chapter of Genesis. Paul is talking about the faith in his heart which he had back in the fifteenth chapter of Genesis.

We find in this chapter that God commands Abraham to offer Isaac on an altar but restrains him when he obeys. Then God confirms His covenant to Abraham.

GOD COMMANDS ABRAHAM TO OFFER ISAAC

And it came to pass after these things, that God did tempt Abraham, and said unto him, Abraham: and he said, Behold, here I am.

And he said, Take now thy son, thine only son Isaac, whom thou lovest, and get thee into the land of Moriah; and offer him there for a burnt-offering upon one of the mountains which I will tell thee of [Gen. 22:1, 2].

The translation "tempt" here may be a little bit too strong. Actually, the word means *to test*. James makes it very clear that God never tempts anyone with evil. God tempts folks in the sense that He tests their faith. What He is doing here is testing Abraham. He asks him to do something that is very strange.

Right after this chapter, the record (23:1) tells us that Sarah was an hundred and seven and twenty years old. So we see that by this time Isaac wasn't just a little boy. Sarah was 90 years old when he was born and chapter 23 begins with her at 127 years of age. So it is probably fair to assume that Isaac was in his thirties at the time he was offered. One can realize then, how it would be a heartbreak for Abraham to take this young man and offer him.

"Take now thy son." Remember that the Lord Jesus is the Son in His position in the Trinity. "Thine only son." The Lord Jesus is called the only begotten Son of the Father. "Thine only son, Isaac, whom thou lovest." The Lord Jesus declared that He was loved by the Father. It is the belief of many that Moriah is the particular mount that the Temple is built on. The Lord Jesus was sacrificed just outside the city walls. When I was in Jerusalem, I realized that Golgotha and the Temple area were not very far apart, and they actually belong to the same ridge that goes through there. It is not so obvious because a street has been cut through it on an old roadway from times past. I think the entire ridge was Moriah. So many people believe that the Lord Jesus died on the same ridge, the same mountain, possibly even on the same spot, where Abraham offered Isaac.

Isaac was to be offered as a burnt offering. The burnt offering was that which was offered to God until the time of the Mosaic Law. Then God told about a sin offering and a trespass offering which were to be made. Here the burnt offering speaks of the person of Christ and who He is.

This whole episode raises a natural question. Isn't it wrong to offer human sacrifice? Of course, it is morally wrong. So let us look at this for a moment. I'm of the opinion that had you met Abraham on that day and asked him where he was going, he would have said he was going to offer Isaac as a sacrifice. Then if you had asked whether he didn't know that was wrong, I think he would have said, "Yes, I've been taught that it is wrong. I know that the heathen nations around here, such as the Philistines who offer to Moloch, all offer human sacrifice, and I have been taught that is wrong." Then if you had asked him why he is doing it anyway, he would have said, "All I know is that God commanded me to do it. I don't understand it, but I have been walking with Him now for 25 years and He has never failed me. He has never asked me to do anything that did not prove to be the best thing. I don't understand this command He has given me, but I believe that if I go all the way with Him, He will raise Isaac from the dead. I believe that is what He will do."

ABRAHAM OBEYS GOD

And Abraham rose up early in the morning, and saddled his ass, and took two of his young men with him, and Isaac his son, and clave the wood for the burnt-offering,

and rose up, and went unto the place of which God had told him

Then on the third day Abraham lifted up his eyes, and saw the place afar off.

And Abraham said unto his young men, Abide ye here with the ass; and I and the lad will go yonder and worship, and come again to you [Gen. 22:3-5].

Here we see how Abraham goes out and takes the boy with him and also takes the wood for the burnt offering. Since it took him three days to get there, it was on the third day that Abraham received him back from the "dead." That is the way Abraham looked at it. He was raised up to Abraham on the third day. What a picture we have here!

Now there is going to take place a transaction here between the father and the son, between Abraham and Isaac. Actually, the same thing happened at the cross. God shut man out at the cross and at the time of the darkness at high noon, man was excluded. The night had come when no man could work and during those last three hours, the cross became an altar on which the Lamb of God who takes away the sin of the world was offered. The transaction was between the Father and the Son on that cross. Man was standing on the outside, not participating at all. We have the same picture here with Isaac and Abraham.

And Abraham took the wood of the burnt-offering, and laid it upon Isaac his son; and he took the fire in his hand, and a knife; and they went both of them together.

And Isaac spake unto Abraham his father, and said, My father: and he said, Here am I, my son. And he said, Behold the fire and the wood: but where is the lamb for a burnt-offering?

And Abraham lifted up his eyes, and looked, and behold behind him a ram caught in a thicket by his horns: and Abraham went and took the ram, and offered him up for a burnt-offering in the stead of his son [Gen. 22:6, 7, 13].

Isaac carried the wood for the offering. Remember that Christ carried his own cross. The fire speaks of judgment and the knife speaks of the execution of judgment, of sacrifice.

People will say that shortly after this a ram got caught in the thicket by his horns and Abraham caught him and offered him. That is right. That is exactly what happened. Abraham said that God Himself would provide a Lamb. There was no *lamb* there. It was a *ram* that was caught — and there is a distinction. The Lamb was not provided until 1900 years later when John the Baptist marked Him out and identified Him by saying, "Behold, the Lamb of God that taketh away the sin of the world."

And Abraham said, My son, God will provide himself a lamb for a burnt-offering: so they went both of them together [Gen. 22:8],

"God will provide Himself a lamb for a burnt offering" — this is very important for us to note at this particular place because Abraham is now ready to offer this boy on the altar. Abraham still does not completely understand it.

And they came to the place which God had told him of; and Abraham built an altar there, and laid the wood in order, and bound Isaac his son, and laid him on the altar upon the wood [Gen. 22:9].

Remember that Isaac is actually a grown man. He is not just a little boy whom Abraham had to tie up. I believe that he could have overcome Abraham if it had come to a physical encounter. But Isaac is doing this in obedience. The Lord Jesus went to the cross to fulfill the will of God. He prayed, "Not My will, but Thine be done." We have a picture of Him here.

And Abraham stretched forth his hand, and took the knife to slay his son [Gen. 22:10].

Again, if you and I had been there, we would be asking Abraham whether he is really going through with this. It looks like God is going to have him really go through with a human sacrifice. I believe Abraham would have answered that he intended to go all the way although he didn't understand why God would ask him to do this which was wrong. He had learned to obey God and in this crisis he would choose to obey God. This is the real crisis in this man's life.

We have been following the crises in the life of Abraham. God has brought this man through some real exercise of soul, some real heartaches. First of all, he was called to leave all his relatives in Ur of the Chaldees. To leave the whole group was a real test for Abraham. He didn't do it very well at the beginning. Nevertheless, the break finally came. Then there was that test that came concerning his nephew Lot. He loved Lot or he wouldn't have been carrying him around with him as he did. The time came when he had to separate from Lot when Lot went down to Sodom.

Then we find he went through the testing with Ishmael. Abraham loved that boy and he cried out to God, "Oh, that Ishmael might live before Thee!" He hated to be separated from that son. Now he comes to this supreme test when he is asked to give up Isaac. He doesn't quite understand all the details about this. God had told him that in Isaac should his seed be called. He could depend on that. He believed that God would raise Isaac from the dead. As far as Abraham is concerned, he is willing to go through with this sacrifice in obedience to God.

James wrote that we can see that Abraham was justified by works when he offered his son. But wait a minute, did he offer his son? Does the Bible say he plunged the knife into his son?

And the angel of the LORD called unto him out of heaven, and said, Abraham, Abraham: and he said, Here am I.

And he said, Lay not thine hand upon the lad, neither do thou any thing unto him: for now I know that thou fearest God, seeing thou hast not withheld thy son, thine only son from me [Gen. 22:11, 12].

Now he knows. How does He know? By action. By works. Before, God knew because he could see Abraham's heart. He knew Abraham's faith. He knew whether or not it was genuine. But Abraham's neighbor couldn't tell. His friends weren't sure. They can only know by works. That is why James says that faith without works is dead. Faith produces something. So God tests Abraham.

May I say that I believe that any person whom God calls, any person whom God saves, any person whom God uses, is going to be tested. God tested Abraham, and today God tests those who are His own. He tests you and me today and He gives us these tests to strengthen our faith, to establish us and make us serviceable for Him. This is the important thing for us to note here. He is giving this man Abraham the supreme test. God will not have to ask anything of him after this.

We have already read the thirteenth verse about the ram which was caught in the thicket. You will notice that there has been a substitution all the way from the Garden of Eden down to the cross of Christ. This little animal pointed to His coming. God would not permit human sacrifice. But when His own Son came into the world, His Son went to the cross and died. God spared not His own Son but delivered Him up for us all (Rom. 8:32).That cross became an altar on which the Lamb of God that taketh away the sin of the world was offered. Do you see that, my friend?

And Abraham called the name of that place Jehovah-jireh: as it is said to this day, In the mount of the LORD it shall be seen [Gen. 22:14].

Abraham names this place. A great many people believe this is where Solomon built the Temple and where Golgotha, the place of the skull, are to be found. It is all the same ridge where Abraham offered his son. It was there that the Lord Jesus Christ was crucified. Abraham called the name of that place Jehovah-jireh, meaning, *Jehovah will provide*. It is here where God intervened in his behalf.

GOD REAFFIRMS HIS ORIGINAL PROMISES TO ABRAHAM

And the angel of the LORD called unto Abraham out of heaven the second time,

And said, By myself have I sworn, saith the LORD, for because thou hast done this thing, and hast not withheld thy son, thine only son:

That in blessing I will bless thee, and in multiplying I will multiply thy seed as the stars of the heaven, and as the

sand which is upon the sea shore; and thy seed shall possess the gate of his enemies:

And in thy seed shall all the nations of the earth be blessed; because thou hast obeyed my voice [Gen. 22:15-18].

God now has a message for him. God said that he did not withhold his son. Did Abraham actually offer his son? No, God didn't make him go all the way through it. But Abraham showed that he believed God and he went far enough to let you and me know, and to let God know, and to let the whole created universe know, that he was willing to give his son. So God counted it as if he had done it. He is justified by his faith. He is also justified before men by his works. He demonstrated that he had that faith.

Notice how God dwells on this. "Hast not withheld thy son, thine only son." God gave His only Son.

God says that all the nations of the earth shall be blessed in his seed. Today the Gospel of Christ has gone to the whole world. There are still some who have not heard, it is true, even in our own country. Nevertheless, the blessing has come to all nations. The only blessing the nations do have is through Christ.

God gave this promise because Abraham had obeyed His voice. That obedience rested upon his faith, and faith will always lead to action. Faith without works is dead.

In the offering of Isaac God is making it clear that there will have to be a man to stand in the gap. There will have to be a man who will be capable of becoming the Saviour if anyone out of the race of mankind is to be saved. That is the great lesson that is given to us in this. God did not let Abraham go through with it because it would have been wrong. God spared Abraham's son, but God did not spare His own Son but gave Him up freely for us all. God provided a ram for Abraham to offer, but 1900 years later God provided the Lamb of God to be offered.

Now, when God promises that "in thy seed shall all the families of the earth be blessed" what is He talking about? What seed? Paul interprets this for us.

Now to Abraham and his seed were the promises made. He saith not, And to seeds, as of many; but as of one, And to thy seed, which is Christ [Gal. 3:16].

You see that the Bible has its own interpretation of this.

And the scripture, foreseeing that God would justify the heathen through faith, preached before the gospel unto Abraham, saying, In thee shall all nations be blessed.

So then they which be of faith are blessed with faithful Abraham [Gal. 3:8, 9].

When did God preach the gospel to Abraham? It was when God called upon him to offer his son Isaac upon the altar. That was the time when God preached the gospel to him because He told him that in his seed all nations should be blessed. That seed is Christ. This is the Gospel that was given to Abraham.

We often assume that Abraham, Isaac, Jacob, and all of those Old Testament saints, were great men but that they were not as informed as we are. We assume they didn't know as much as we know. I'm of the opinion that Abraham knew a great deal more about the coming of Christ and the Gospel than we realize. In fact, the Lord Jesus said,

Your father Abraham rejoiced to see my day and he saw it, and was glad [John 8:56].

God revealed a great deal to Abraham. God preached the Gospel to Abraham. The Saviour had not yet come, but here on Mt. Moriah God taught Abraham through the offering of Isaac which is a picture of the offering of Christ and even of His resurrection. This occurred three days after God had asked him to offer Isaac, and God gave him back to Abraham alive on the third day. This pictures the death and resurrection of Christ, and is the reason Paul says that God preached the Gospel to Abraham.

ABRAHAM RETURNS TO BEER-SHEBA

So Abraham returned unto his young men, and they rose up and went together to Beer-sheba; and Abraham dwelt at Beer-sheba.

And it came to pass after these things, that it was told Abraham, saying, Behold, Milcah, she hath also born children unto thy brother Nahor [Gen. 22:19, 20].

Here we find a little insight into the family of Abraham. He had left his relatives back yonder in the land of Haran, and this is just a little sidelight on that family. This line will not be followed in the Scripture, but it will cross the line of Abraham a little later, which is the reason it is important and included here. You will find that reading the rest of this chapter is quite a little exercise in the pronunciation of names.

CHAPTER 23

The chapter tells of the death of Sarah and of Abraham's purchase of a cave in which to bury her, the cave of Machpelah.

DEATH OF SARAH

And Sarah was an hundred and seven and twenty years old: these were the years of the life of Sarah.

And Sarah died in Kirjath-arba; the same is Hebron in the land of Canaan: and Abraham came to mourn for Sarah, and to weep for her [Gen. 23:1, 2].

Sarah is stated to be 127 years old. Since she was 90 when Isaac was born, he would have been 37 years old at the time of her death. I would suppose that this was a few years after the incident of the offering of Isaac.

Sarah died in Kirjatharba which is Hebron in the land of Canaan. We'll notice that Abraham had to *buy* a cave in which to bury his dead in the very land that God had *given* to him. Why didn't he take her somewhere else to bury her? It is because their hope of the future is in that land. These arrangements for a funeral are not very interesting, maybe even a little morbid for some of us, but it is important to see the truth taught here.

ABRAHAM BUYS FIELD OF EPHRON IN MACHPELAH FROM SONS OF HETH

And Abraham stood up from before his dead, and spake' unto the sons of Heth, saying,

I am a stranger and a sojourner with you: give me a possession of a buryingplace with you, that I may bury my dead out of my sight.

And the children of Heth answered Abraham, saying unto him,

> **Hear us, my lord: thou art a mighty prince among us: in the choice of our sepulchres bury thy dead; none of us shall withhold from thee his sepulchre, but that thou mayest bury thy dead** [Gen. 23:3-6].

Abraham calls himself a stranger and a sojourner even in the land which God had promised to give him. The children of Heth who lived in this land made a very generous offer to him. You see, Abraham was a mighty prince, and his influence had counted for something.

> **And Abraham stood up, and bowed himself to the people of the land, even to the children of Heth.**
>
> **And he communed with them, saying, If it be your mind that I should bury my dead out of my sight; hear me, and intreat for me to Ephron the son of Zohar,**
>
> **That he may give me the cave of Machpelah, which he hath, which is in the end of his field; for as much money as it is worth he shall give it me for a possession of a buryingplace amongst you** [Gen. 23:7-9].

The cave of Machpelah was the place Abraham wanted, but he insisted upon buying it. He wanted nothing given to him. In other words, until God gave him that land he would buy what he needed and what he wanted. He buys a buryingplace.

We are going to find as we go through the Bible that there are two great hopes and two great purposes which God has. He has an earthly purpose and He has a heavenly purpose. He has an earthly purpose; that is, this earth in which you and I live is going into eternity. It is going to be a new model. There will be a new heaven and a new earth, but there is going to be an *earth*, and it will be inhabited throughout eternity. That was the hope of Abraham. Abraham wanted to be buried in that land so that when the resurrection came, he and Sarah would be raised in that land. He didn't know how many would be coming after him, but there are going to be literally millions raised from the dead. That is their hope. It is an earthly hope and it will be realized.

When our Lord was in the Upper Room with His disciples who were schooled in the Old Testament, having the Old Testament hope, He said to them, "Let not your heart be troubled; ye believe in God, believe also in Me. In My Father's house are many abiding places . . . I go to prepare a place for you. And if I go and prepare a place for you, I'll come again, and receive you unto Myself, that where I am, there ye may be also" (John 14:1-3). That is the new Jerusalem. It is something that He is preparing today, and it is the place where the church is going. It will be the eternal abode of the church. That was brand-new to His disciples, and I'm afraid it is brand-new to a great many Christians today. God never told Abraham that He was going to take him away from this earth to heaven. He kept telling Abraham that He was going to give him this land. Abraham believed God and this is the reason he wants to bury Sarah in that land. And he is buried there at Hebron also.

We made a trip down there, and over that spot today there is a Mohammedan mosque. Frankly, I never felt uncomfortable or afraid in that entire land except at Hebron. We had been warned to be very careful in Hebron because there is a great deal of antagonism against the tourists — in fact, a great deal of antagonism to practically everyone who did not belong there. Of course, they let us into the mosque because it means tourist dollars. One looks down through a little hole in the floor, down into the cave. Sarah and Abraham, Isaac and Rebecca, and Jacob and Leah are supposed to be there (Rachel is buried on up at Bethlehem). They had a hope of being raised from the dead in that land. They have an earthly hope. Our hope is an heavenly hope. I trust this is made clear to you today so that you can see the importance of this section of scripture. That is the reason it is given in so much detail here at this particular time.

So Abraham must make a deal to buy the cave. Notice the transaction.

> **And Ephron dwelt among the children of Heth: and Ephron the Hittite answered Abraham in the audience of the children of Heth, even of all that went in at the gate of his city, saying,**
>
> **Nay, my lord, hear me: the field give I thee, and the cave that is therein, I give it thee; in the presence of the sons of my people give I it thee: bury thy dead.**

> And Abraham bowed down himself before the people of the land.
>
> And he spake unto Ephron in the audience of the people of the land, saying, But if thou wilt give it, I pray thee, hear me: I will give thee money for the field; take it of me, and I will bury my dead there.
>
> And Ephron answered Abraham, saying unto him,
>
> My lord, hearken unto me: the land is worth four hundred shekels of silver; what is that betwixt me and thee? bury therefore thy dead [Gen. 23:10-15].

They certainly were polite in that day. Some folk have the impression these were cave men who clubbed each other, but if Abraham, Isaac, Jacob, and the Old Testament saints would come to our cities today, I think they would go back to report to their folk that the modern man is highly uncivilized — rude and crude and a disgrace. I think they would say that about us today. But we have the advantage. We can talk about them. It is interesting to notice how polite they were.

> And Abraham hearkened unto Ephron; and Abraham weighed to Ephron the silver, which he had named in the audience of the sons of Heth, four hundred shekels of silver, current money with the merchant.
>
> And the field of Ephron, which was in Machpelah, which was before Mamre, the field, and the cave which was therein, and all the trees that were in the field, that were in all the borders round about, were made sure
>
> Unto Abraham for a possession in the presence of the children of Heth, before all that went in at the gate of his city [Gen. 23:16-18].

Abraham payed in the legal tender of that day.

BURIAL OF SARAH

> And after this, Abraham buried Sarah his wife in the cave of the field of Machpelah before Mamre: the same is Hebron in the land of Canaan.

And the field, and the cave that is therein, were made sure unto Abraham for a possession of a buryingplace by the sons of Heth [Gen. 23:19, 20].

Apparently this is the place in Hebron where the mosque stands today. By the way, it is considered either the second or the third most important mosque of the world of Islam. They have many beautiful mosques in Cairo and other places, but the most important one is at Mecca; then either the one in Jerusalem or the one in Hebron ranks next. You can see how important this is because the Arab also traces his lineage back to Abraham.

CHAPTER 24

We have completed the section which tells of Abraham, the man of faith. Now we come to the life of Isaac, the beloved son.

This chapter tells how Abraham sends his trusted servant to get a bride for Isaac in Mesopotamia and the success of the servant in securing Rebekah. This is one of those beautiful chapters of the Bible. It tells a very beautiful story. This love story will reveal again that God is interested in the man whom you marry, young lady, and He is interested in the young lady whom you marry, young man. God is interested in your *love* story, and it is wonderful when you bring God into it. You will find that the first miracle our Lord performed was when He went to a wedding in Cana of Galilee. I don't know how many weddings He attended, but we do know He went to that one. And He would like to go to yours.

ABRAHAM INSTRUCTS SERVANT TO GO TO MESOPOTAMIA TO GET BRIDE FOR ISAAC

And Abraham was old, and well stricken in age: and the LORD had blessed Abraham in all things [Gen. 24:1].

Now this old man wants to get a bride for his son, Isaac, but he doesn't want to get a bride in that section where the people were given to idolatry and lived in paganism. He wants a bride from among His people, back in the land of Haran.

There are three great events in the life of Isaac, and we have already seen two of them. One is his birth. The second is his offering by Abraham. The third event is the securing of his bride. There are three great events in the life of any man: his birth, his marriage, and his death. And man has no choice except in the middle one — sometimes he does not even have much choice in that one.

In this chapter, telling us of the choice of a bride for Isaac, I want you to notice two truths as we go through it. One truth to note is the leading of the Lord in all the details of the lives of those involved. Even in this early day there were those in that social climate who were looking to God and following His leading. This is supposed to be way back in the stone age when man was a cave man and uncivilized. Don't believe a word of it. Early man was not that kind of a man at all. We find him here being led of God. If God could lead back in that day in the lives of those folks, then He can lead today in your life and in my life. This puts down a pattern for us.

The second thing to notice is the straightforward manner in which Rebekah made her decision to go with the servant and become the bride of Isaac.

And Abraham said unto his eldest servant of his house, that ruled over all that he had, Put, I pray thee, thy hand under my thigh:

And I will make thee swear by the LORD, the God of heaven, and the God of the earth, that thou shalt not take a wife unto my son of the daughters of the Canaanites, among whom I dwell [Gen. 24:2, 3].

This was the way men took an oath in that day. They didn't raise their right hand and put their left hand on a Bible. They didn't have a Bible to begin with, and frankly, if it is necessary to do that to get you to tell the truth, then it is very possible you wouldn't tell the truth anyway. But the method used in that day was to put one's hand on the thigh of the man to whom he is going to make an oath. I think the servant was probably Eliezer because we know he was the head servant in the home of Abraham.

My Christian friend, if you have a boy or a girl in your home and they are of the marriageable age, you ought to pray that they will not marry one of the "Canaanites" — they are still in the land. If they do, as someone has said, you are going to have the devil for a father-in-law. There will be trouble. There always is trouble and heartache.

But thou shalt go unto my country, and to my kindred, and take a wife unto my son Isaac.

And the servant said unto him, Peradventure the woman will not be willing to follow me unto this land: must I needs bring thy son again unto the land from whence thou camest?

And Abraham said unto him, Beware thou that thou bring not my son thither again [Gen. 24:4-6].

The servant wonders whether he should come back and get Isaac and take him to that land in case he can't find a girl that will come with him. Abraham tells him never to take Isaac away. This is the place where God wants Abraham and Isaac, and He doesn't want them to return back to that land under any circumstance. It is very important to see that.

The LORD God of heaven, which took me from my father's house, and from the land of my kindred, and which spake unto me, and that sware unto me, saying, Unto thy seed will I give this land; he shall send his angel before thee, and thou shalt take a wife unto my son from thence [Gen. 24:7].

Abraham is really a man of faith. He demonstrates it again and again and here he is magnificent. He tells his servant that he can count on God to lead him. God has promised this to Abraham. You see, he is not taking a leap into the dark. Faith is never a leap into the dark; it must rest upon the Word of God.

God had made a contract with him which is why he can say that God had promised him that through his seed, that is, through Isaac, He is going to bring a blessing to the world. So he can be absolutely sure of one thing — God has a bride back there for Isaac. You see, he rests upon what God had said.

We do not need to be foolish today. Faith is not foolishness if it rests upon the Word of God. It is always reasonable. It is never a leap in the dark. It is not a gamble. It is not betting your life that this or that will come to pass. It is a sure thing. And the faith of Abraham here is sure.

And if the woman will not be willing to follow thee, then thou shalt be clear from this my oath: only bring not my son thither again [Gen. 24:8].

"If the woman will not come, then you are discharged from your errand, but don't ever return my son back there." Now what does that mean? I think that Abraham would have told you very frankly, "Then God has another way of finding the right bride for Isaac."

Friends, that is what faith is. Faith is acting upon the Word of God. It rests upon something. God wants us to believe *His Word* and not just believe. Abraham had something to rest upon. He is not demanding something of God. And he is confident that if this plan doesn't work, then God has another way to accomplish His will.

And the servant put his hand under the thigh of Abraham his master, and sware to him concerning that matter [Gen. 24:9].

THE SERVANT GOES ON THE MISSION OF SEEKING BRIDE FOR ISAAC

And the servant took ten camels of the camels of his master, and departed; for all the goods of his master were in his hand: and he arose, and went to Mesopotamia, unto the city of Nahor [Gen. 24:10].

Let me digress to make this comment. Three wise men who came in on three camels to Jerusalem when Jesus was born wouldn't have created a stir in the city. I believe there were nearer three hundred wise men and their camels. The Scripture does not give any number, of course, nor does it mention the number of gifts. It simply states that there were three kinds of gifts, but that doesn't confine it to three wise men. You'll notice here when there were only the servants going to Mesopotamia to get a bride for Isaac, that there were ten camels which probably means there were ten servants that went. So this was quite a retinue of servants.

It states that all the goods of his master were in his hand. He had charge of all the chattel and all the possessions of Abraham.

And he made his camels to kneel down without the city by a well of water at the time of the evening, even the time that women go out to draw water.

And he said, O LORD God of my master Abraham, I pray thee, send me good speed this day, and shew kindness unto my master Abraham.

Behold, I stand here by the well of water; and the daughters of the men of the city come out to draw water:

And let it come to pass, that the damsel to whom I shall say, Let down thy pitcher, I pray thee, that I may drink; and she shall say, Drink, and I will give thy camels drink also: let the same be she that thou hast appointed for thy servant Isaac; and thereby shall I know that thou hast shewed kindness unto my master [Gen. 24:11-14].

It may seem strange to you that the women came out to draw water, but they were the ones who did the watering of the camels in that day. Very frankly, women did lots more work in those days then they do today — I mean hard, physical work. The women were the ones who watered the stock and took care of them. The men were supposed to be out trading, of course, and they were supposed to be out doing other work. They weren't always loafing, by any means, but it is interesting to note that it was the custom for the women to go out to draw water. When a servant came, it was not the proper thing for him, as a stranger, to water his camels before the folk who lived in that community.

Notice here how the servant of Abraham is depending on God. Abraham had put this whole affair into the hands of this servant. So the servant prays to God. He tells God that he wouldn't know which one to choose out of these girls. So he prays that he might choose the one whom God has already chosen. In other words, he asks the Lord to lead him in making the right choice.

He's going to ask one of them to give him a drink. Now whom do you think he's going to choose? Well, he's a man. He's going to pick the best looking one who comes out. You can be sure that Rebekah was a good-looking woman. The Puritans had the idea that beauty was of the devil. Well, the devil is beautiful because the Bible calls him and angel of light, but he doesn't possess all beauty. After all, God is the Creator, and you have never seen a lovely sunset or looked at a beautiful flower that didn't come from the hands of the Creator. It is God who makes women beautiful. There's nothing wrong with that. So this man is going to choose the beautiful one. He'd be a pretty poor servant if he didn't, I'll tell you that.

THE SERVANT MEETS REBEKAH AT WELL

> And it came to pass, before he had done speaking, that, behold, Rebekah came out, who was born to Bethuel, son of Milcah, the wife of Nahor, Abraham's brother, with her pitcher upon her shoulder.

> And the damsel was very fair to look upon, a virgin, neither had any man known her: and she went down to the well, and filled her pitcher, and came up [Gen. 24:15, 16].

Here is the one. I told you she was good looking, because the Word of God says that she was. I resent the fact that beauty is associated with the entertainment world and the devil today. I think that the Lord ought to have some of that beauty. He made it to begin with, and there is nothing wrong with God using a beautiful person. I always pray that God will call fine-looking men and women into His service today. This Rebekah was not just an ordinary girl. She was fair to look upon and could have won the beauty contest.

> And the servant ran to meet her, and said, Let me, I pray thee, drink a little water of thy pitcher.

> And she said, Drink, my lord: and she hasted, and let down her pitcher upon her hand, and gave him drink.

> And when she had done giving him drink, she said, I will draw water for thy camels also, until they have done drinking.

> And she hasted, and emptied her pitcher into the trough, and ran again unto the well to draw water, and drew for all his camels [Gen. 24:17-20].

Notice here that this girl is not only beautiful, but she is also very courteous and polite. She was willing to work and be helpful. Remember that there were *ten* of those camels!

And the man wondering at her held his peace, to wit whether the LORD had made his journey prosperous or not.

And it came to pass, as the camels had done drinking, that the man took a golden earring of half a shekel weight, and two bracelets for her hands of ten shekels weight of gold;

And said, Whose daughter art thou? tell me, I pray thee: is there room in thy father's house for us to lodge in?

And she said unto him, I am the daughter of Bethuel the son of Milcah, which she bare unto Nahor.

She said moreover unto him, We have both straw and provender enough, and room to lodge in.

And the man bowed down his head, and worshipped the LORD [Gen. 24:21-26].

You see, the servant just stands there in amazement. He had been wondering if she was the one, and whether God was leading or not. When he finds out about her family, and realizes she is the daughter of Nahor's son, and Nahor is the brother of Abraham, then he sees the hand of God in it all. It is wonderful to have God leading and guiding, isn't it?

And he said, Blessed be the LORD God of my master Abraham, who hath not left destitute my master of his mercy and his truth: I being in the way, the LORD led me to the house of my master's brethren [Gen. 24:27].

The Lord leads those who are in the way, that is, who are in *His* way, who are wanting to be led by Him, and will do what He wants done. God can lead a willing heart anytime.

And the damsel ran, and told them of her mother's house these things.

And Rebekah had a brother, and his name was Laban: and Laban ran out unto the man, unto the well.

And it came to pass, when he saw the earring and bracelets upon his sister's hands, and when he heard the

words of Rebekah his sister, saying, Thus spake the man unto me; that he came unto the man; and, behold, he stood by the camels at the well [Gen. 24:28-30].

Right here we are introduced to Brother Laban and later on he'll be Uncle Laban. Keep your eye on him. He'll bear watching at this point and from here on. He was greatly impressed by the material things, you will notice.

The servant just waited out there at the well to see whether anyone would come out to lead him into the home of Rebekah. He didn't know whether he was really welcome or not. Believe me, when Laban saw those rings, he knew this was a very wealthy guest, and old Laban is not missing a deal. If you doubt that, you ask Jacob later on. Jacob found out that Uncle Laban was a real trader. In fact, he was a better trader than Jacob was. So here, Laban goes out to welcome the wealthy guest.

THE SERVANT INVITED INTO HOME OF BETHUEL, FATHER OF REBEKAH

And he said, Come in, thou blessed of the LORD; wherefore standest thou without? for I have prepared the house, and room for the camels.

And the man came into the house: and he ungirded his camels, and gave straw and provender for the camels, and water to wash his feet, and the men's feet that were with him [Gen. 24:31, 32].

Laban recognized the fact that there was a living God, the Creator, and he blesses the servant and welcomes him. We notice the foot-washing ceremony again, and we notice that there were quite a few men with the servant. They are entertained royally; Uncle Laban sees to that.

Then we go into the dramatic story of how this servant wins Rebekah, and asks her to go home with him to Isaac.

THE SERVANT STATES HIS MISSION

And there was set meat before him to eat: but he said, I will not eat, until I have told mine errand. And he said, Speak on [Gen. 24:33].

We are having presented to us here a marvelous picture of the relationship of Christ and the church. One of the figures of speech used in the New Testament is that the church is to become the bride of Christ someday. This is the way the church is being won today: the Father and the Son have sent the Holy Spirit into the world. The Spirit of God, like the servant, has to come to talk about Another. He takes the things of Christ and shows them to us. As this servant has gone to get a bride for Isaac, so the Spirit of God is in the world to call out a bride for Christ. That is why this story is so dramatic and marvelous. We don't want to miss any of the excitement of it.

The servant of Abraham says that he cannot eat until he has told them his mission. The Holy Spirit has come into the world to tell us about another One, which is the primary business as far as God is concerned. I know that there are other businesses that are very important. The business of our government, the business of getting out the news, the great corporations like the automobile and airplane industries, all of this is great business and is important. But, very frankly, friends, God is not continuing to deal with this world because of General Motors or the government in Washington, whether Democrat or Republican. That's not primary in heaven. And the stock market on Wall Street is of no great concern in heaven. The thing that is primary, as far as God is concerned, is to get out the Gospel. This servant wouldn't even eat before he could give his message. And the Spirit of God is in the world today to give us a message.

And he said, I am Abraham's servant [Gen. 24:34].

He doesn't give his name. The Lord Jesus said that when the Holy Spirit comes, He will not speak of Himself but He will take the things of Christ and will show them to us. By the way, what is the name of the Holy Spirit? He has no name. He doesn't come to speak of Himself. He comes to speak of another, namely Christ.

And the LORD hath blessed my master greatly; and he is become great: and he hath given him flocks, and herds, and silver, and gold, and menservants, and maidservants, and camels, and asses [Gen. 24:35].

How wonderful! *My* Father is also rich today. Rich in cattle. Rich in goods. The cattle on a thousand hills are His. How great the Father is!

And Sarah my master's wife bare a son to my master when she was old: and unto him hath he given all that he hath [Gen. 24:36].

The Lord Jesus is the Inheritor. And we are the joint heirs with Him today. The servant tells this family that he is after a bride for his master's son, and the son is going to inherit all things.

And my master made me swear, saying, Thou shalt not take a wife to my son of the daughters of the Canaanites, in whose land I dwell:

But thou shalt go unto my father's house, and to my kindred, and take a wife unto my son [Gen. 24:37, 38].

Friends, the Holy Spirit is calling out sinners — but they are sinners who are born again, "not of corruptible seed but of incorruptible seed, by the Word of God that liveth and abideth forever." Those are the ones He is calling out. They are sinners but they have been made the children of God. If any man be in Christ Jesus, he is a new creature. This servant is not taking someone of the unregenerate Canaanites.

And I said unto my master, Peradventure the woman will not follow me.

And he said unto me, The LORD, before whom I walk, will send his angel with thee, and prosper thy way; and thou shalt take a wife for my son of my kindred, and of my father's house:

Then shalt thou be clear from this my oath, when thou comest to my kindred; and if they give not thee one, thou shalt be clear from my oath.

And I came this day unto the well, and said, O LORD God of my master Abraham, if now thou do prosper my way which I go:

Behold, I stand by the well of water: and it shall come to pass, that when the virgin cometh forth to draw water,

and I say to her, Give me, I pray thee, a little water of thy pitcher to drink;

And she say to me, Both drink thou, and I will also draw for thy camels: let the same be the woman whom the LORD hath appointed out for my master's son.

And before I had done speaking in mine heart, behold, Rebekah came forth with her pitcher on her shoulder; and she went down unto the well, and drew water: and I said unto her, Let me drink, I pray thee.

And she made haste, and let down her pitcher from her shoulder and said, Drink, and I will give thy camels drink also: so I drank, and she made the camels drink also.

And I asked her, and said, Whose daughter art thou? And she said, The daughter of Bethuel, Nahor's son, whom Milcah bare unto him: and I put the earring upon her face, and the bracelets upon her hands.

And I bowed down my head, and worshipped the LORD, and blessed the LORD God of my master Abraham, which had led me in the right way to take my master's brother's daughter unto his son.

And now if ye will deal kindly and truly with my master, tell me: and if not, tell me; that I may turn to the right hand, or to the left [Gen. 24:39-49].

PERMISSION GRANTED TO REBEKAH TO BECOME BRIDE OF ISAAC

Laban acts as the spokesman for this family. He says that as far as they are concerned, this is of the Lord and Rebekah may go.

Then Laban and Bethuel answered and said, The thing proceedeth from the Lord: we cannot speak unto thee bad or good.

Behold, Rebekah is before thee, take her, and go, and let her be thy master's son's wife, as the LORD hath spoken.

And it came to pass, that, when Abraham's servant heard their words, he worshipped the LORD, bowing himself to the earth.

And the servant brought forth jewels of silver, and the jewels of gold, and raiment, and gave them to Rebekah: he gave also to her brother and to her mother precious things [Gen. 24:50-53].

For the believer today the Holy Spirit brings wonderful gifts. We are regenerated, indwelt, baptized, and given the earnest of the Spirit when we come to Christ, having been justified by faith.

And they did eat and drink, he and the men that were with him, and tarried all night; and they rose up in the morning, and he said, Send me away unto my master.

And her brother and her mother said, Let the damsel abide with us a few days, at the least ten: after that she shall go [Gen. 24:54, 55].The very next morning this ser-

The very next morning this servant wanted to be on his way. I'll tell you, this is big business for him. The others weren't in such a hurry, and they wanted to keep Rebekah at least ten days longer so they could talk this all over with her.

And he said unto them, Hinder me not, seeing the LORD hath propsered my way: send me away that I may go to my master.

And they said, We will call the damsel, and inquire at her mouth [Gen. 24:56, 57].

Now we come to an important part, and it is really very wonderful. Don't miss this!

And they called Rebekah, and said unto her, Wilt thou go with this man? And she said, I will go [Gen. 24:58].

Let's go back and look at this picture again. It is an oriental scene, couched way back yonder about 4,000 years ago. Here is this family entertaining a guest, a stranger, and they are entertaining him royally. They had fed his camels, taken care of the servants, set a meal before him, and he wanted to state his business. He did. He told his strange business. He talks about the master's house.

The Spirit of God would also have us know about the Father's house. When He comes, He will convict the world of sin, of righteousness, and of judgment. Those are the three things that he talks to the lost world about. He tells that the judgment is upon a sinful earth and upon mankind, and that today men are lost because they are sinners. I hear it said today that men are lost because they reject Christ. They are not lost because they reject Christ. They are lost because they are sinners, whether they have heard about Him or not. They are lost sinners. This is our condition today, and this is the condition of all men. The Holy Spirit is coming to let us know that there is a Saviour who has borne our judgment, and He's been made over to us *righteousness*. We have a standing in heaven. He has come to speak to us about that through Christ.

Then the servant told how he had come to get a bride for his master's son Isaac. I can see this servant as he brings out the gifts he is giving to the family — gold and silver, and trinkets. Abraham, you must remember, was a very rich man. The servant is displaying this.

Then he begins to tell about the master. As he does this, I can see in that family circle a very beautiful girl in the background, watching with those deep brown eyes. She's listening, and you can tell she's listening. As she listens, she hears the servant tell about Abraham. He tells how Isaac was born, about the miraculous birth that it was. He tells about his life. Then he tells about the day the father took Isaac up to the top of Mt. Moriah to offer him as a sacrifice, and how God spared Isaac, would not take his life, but gave him back to live with his father.

Now the father has sent *him*, a servant, to get a bride. They don't want to get one back there among the Canaanites. They want to find one that must be of like mind, one who has the same capacity for the living God. She must be born again by the Word of God. He's looking for a bride, and Rebekah is listening all the while. The transaction goes on with the family.

Now they turn to her and all eyes are on her. No one has paid much attention to her up to this point, but now all eyes are on her. They ask her whether she will go. "Rebekah, what about it? Will you go with this man?" She doesn't hedge or hesitate. She says, "I will go."

Have you ever noticed the men whom the Lord Jesus called when He was here on earth? They left their nets and followed Him. Oh, I know, they went back a couple of times, but there came a day when they broke loose from those nets and they never went back to them. They followed Him. They went with Him. He is still calling today. The Holy Spirit is the One who takes the servant's place. The Father and the Spirit sent the Son into the world to die for the human family, and the Son said that when He went back up to heaven, He would send the Holy Spirit, the Comforter. The Holy Spirit has come into the world now, and He is calling out the bride.

He is asking *you*, "Will you go?" Here is the One who died for you. He will save you. You must come to Him as a sinner, which is your rightful position, and accept Him as Saviour. When you do that, you will be born again. You will become a child of God. You will be placed into the church which is going to be presented to Christ someday as a bride. The question is, "Will you go?" Will you trust Christ as your Saviour? Will you accept the invitation? Don't beat around the bush about this. You either accept or you don't.

On one occasion when I was speaking in Texas, I presented Christ and asked, "Will you accept Him?" I wasn't really through preaching, but I shall never forget a young man (I could tell all along he was interested) who got up immediately and walked to the front. It had a tremendous effect upon the audience. He wasn't wishy-washy. There was nothing uncertain about him. My, I love a clean-cut decision like that! That is the way God wants you, friends; that is the way He'll accept you. It is the only way that He'll accept you.

And they sent away Rebekah their sister, and her nurse, and Abraham's servant, and his men.

And they blessed Rebekah, and said unto her, Thou art our sister, be thou the mother of thousands of millions, and let thy seed possess the gate of those which hate them [Gen. 24:59, 60].

That has been fulfilled. We are not talking about unfulfilled prophecy here because that has already been fulfilled. This is not the end of the story either. They start out now to go back to the Promised Land.

THE SERVANT AND REBEKAH BEGIN LONG JOURNEY TO LAND OF PROMISE

And Rebekah arose, and her damsels, and they rode upon the camels, and followed the man: and the servant took Rebekah, and went his way [Gen. 24:61].

Notice that they had a long trip back, but we are not told anything about the trip. It's not easy riding a camel. I rode one from the little village outside of Cairo down to the pyramids, and friends, that is as far as I want to ride on a camel. They call them the ships of the desert. Well, it is as rough as any trip I've ever had on a boat. It was rough. Imagine riding on those camels across the desert!

They would have a hard day on the hot desert, and in the evening they would stop at an oasis, build a campfire and have their evening meal. They would be sitting there before it was time to go to sleep, and I think Rebekah would ask the servant to tell her again about Isaac. The servant would ask her what she would like to hear. And I think she would ask to hear again how he was born and the way his father offered him on the altar. The servant would say, "I told you that last night." But she would want it told again, and again, and again. At night she would have that sweet sleep, dreaming of the time when she'll meet this one. It's a long, hard trip. Maybe her anticipation made the camel not quite so rough, the way not quite so long, and the desert not quite so hot. Finally they come in sight of the land of promise and enter it.

And Isaac came from the way of the well Lahai-roi, for he dwelt in the south country [Gen. 24:62].

This is down in the pleasant country near Hebron and Beersheba.

REBEKAH MEETS ISAAC AND BECOMES HIS BRIDE

> **And Isaac went out to meditate in the field at the eventide: and he lifted up his eyes, and saw, and, behold, the camels were coming [Gen. 24:63].**

Here is a different view of the coming of Christ. So many today are saying that it will be wonderful when the Lord comes and we will be caught up with Him in the air. Well, there is another view, and that is to be with Him when He comes. Most of the church has already gone through the doorway of death, and they will be coming with Him when He comes. Then the bodies will be raised, and the spirit and the bodies will be reunited. Then those who are alive and remain unto the coming of the Lord, are to be caught up with the dead, caught up to meet the Lord in the air. Those who have gone before in death will see Christ when He arises from the right hand of the Father, when He comes to call His church and to meet His church in the air. This is the picture, and what a glorious picture it is!

> **And Rebekah lifted up her eyes, and when she saw Isaac, she lighted off the camel.**
>
> **For she had said unto the servant, What man is this that walketh in the field to meet us? And the servant had said, It is my master: therefore she took a vail, and covered herself [Gen. 24:64, 65].**

The bride of Christ must be clothed with the righteousness of Christ. *He* has been made our righteousness. He was delivered for our offenses, and He was raised for our justification. That was done so that we might have a righteousness that would enable us to stand before God.

In the meantime the Holy Spirit is to reveal Christ and to make Him real to our hearts as we travel this pilgrim pathway. Christian friend, if the road is rough and the way seems long, permit the Holy Spirit to refresh you with the old, old story of Jesus and His love. "Whom having not seen, ye love; in whom, though now ye see him not, yet believing, ye rejoice with joy unspeakable and full of glory" (I Pet. 1:8). What a glorious, wonderful, beautiful picture this is before us here.

And the servant told Isaac all things that he had done.

And Isaac brought her into his mother Sarah's tent, and took Rebekah, and she became his wife; and he loved her: and Isaac was comforted after his mother's death [Gen. 24:66, 67].

As this servant accomplished his mission to get the bride to Isaac, so the Holy Spirit will deliver us to our Bridegroom at the day of redemption. We have been sealed unto the day of redemption.

Notice that Isaac loved her. He was comforted after his mother's death. Christ loved the church and gave Himself for her. This reveals to us that Christ gains a great deal in our salvation. He wants us. He longs for us. Oh, that you and I today might be faithful to Him, my beloved.

CHAPTER 25

This is another great chapter of the Bible. It records the death of Abraham and the birth of the twins, Esau and Jacob, to Isaac and Rebekah. It gives the generations of Ishmael and also the generations of Isaac. Then there is the incident relative to the birthright. So this is a remarkable chapter and it covers a great deal of ground.

This chapter will be the last mention of Abraham, but, frankly, his story ended back in chapter 23 when he sent the servant out to get a bride for Isaac.

ABRAHAM MARRIED KETURAH AND HAS MORE SONS

Then again Abraham took a wife and her name was Keturah.

And she bare him Zimran, and Jokshan, and Medan, and Midian, and Ishbak, and Shuah [Gen. 25:1, 2].

Now he has quite a family. He had his biggest family after the death of Sarah. Somebody will raise the question, "I thought that at the time of the birth of Isaac, Abraham was dead as far as his capability of bringing a child into the world." Granted, he was. But when God does something, He really does it. This is the reason I believe that anything God does bears His signature. Right here, this man Abraham was not only able to bring Isaac into the world, but he now brings in this great family of children.

The interesting thing that we have before us here is the mention of Medan and Midian. The other boys will have nations come from them, but I can't identify them, and I'm not interested in them because they do not cross our pathway in Scripture. But Midian does. We will find later that Moses goes down into the land of Midian and takes a wife there. Remember Midianites are in the line of Abraham; so are the Medanites. So we find here the fact that there are other sons of Abraham, but the Lord has said it is through Isaac that Abraham's seed is called — not through any of these sons. It is not through Ishmael, nor through Midian, nor Medan. All of these were nomads of the desert.

ABRAHAM STILL IDENTIFIES ISAAC AS THE CHOSEN SON, ABRAHAM DIES

And Abraham gave all that he had unto Isaac.

But unto the sons of the concubines, which Abraham had, Abraham gave gifts, and sent them away from Isaac his son, while he yet lived, eastward, unto the east country.

And these are the days of the years of Abraham's life which he lived, an hundred threescore and fifteen years.

Then Abraham gave up the ghost, and died in a good old age, an old man, and full of years; and was gathered to his people.

And his sons Isaac and Ishmael buried him in the cave of Machpelah, in the field of Ephron the son of Zohar the Hittite, which is before Mamre;

The field which Abraham purchased of the sons of Heth: there was Abraham buried, and Sarah his wife.

And it came to pass after the death of Abraham, that God blessed his son Isaac; and Isaac dwelt by the well Lahai-roi [Gen. 25:5-11].

Ishmael comes for the funeral because, after all, Abraham is his father. So Isaac and Ishmael together bury Abraham. Then Isaac goes down to live at the place where he first met Rebekah.

GENERATIONS OF ISHMAEL

In verses 12 to 18 we have the generations of Ishmael, Abraham's son, whom Hagar the Egyptian, Sarah's handmaid, bare unto Abraham. The list of them is given here. I call to your attention again the fact that the Holy Spirit uses this method in the book of Genesis. The rejected line is given first and then set aside and not mentioned any more. Then the line that is leading to Christ is given and followed. So it is after the line of Ishmael is given that we come to the line of Isaac.

RECORD OF ISAAC RESUMED AND BIRTH OF ESAU AND JACOB

And these are the generations of Isaac, Abraham's son: Abraham begat Isaac [Gen. 25:19].

This is the line we are going to follow. Abraham begat Isaac, and Isaac begat Jacob. This is the way the first chapter of Matthew begins. Each of these men had other sons, as we have seen. Abraham had quite a few sons, but the genealogy of those men is not followed. It is the genealogy of Isaac that is followed. You can forget Ishmael, and Midian, and Medan, and all the rest. They will cross paths with the descendants of Isaac time and again, but we will not follow their line.

And Isaac was forty years old when he took Rebekah to wife, the daughter of Bethuel the Syrian of Padan-aram, the sister to Laban the Syrian.

And Isaac intreated the LORD for his wife, because she was barren: and the LORD was intreated of him, and Rebekah his wife conceived.

And the children struggled together within her; and she said, If it be so, why am I thus? And she went to enquire of the LORD [Gen. 25:20-22].

Rebekah was barren but Isaac intreated the Lord and now she is going to give birth to twins. This is an interesting statement that she felt the struggle within her. You will find that it is the struggle that goes on today in the world. There is a struggle today between light and darkness, and between good and evil. There is a struggle between the spirit and the flesh. Every child of God knows something of that struggle which is set before us in the seventh chapter of Romans. Rebekah didn't understand what it was.

And the LORD said unto her, Two nations are in thy womb, and two manner of people shall be separated from thy bowels; and the one people shall be stronger than the other people; and the elder shall serve the younger [Gen. 25:23].

God makes the statement to her that the elder shall serve the younger. She should have believed it, and her younger son should have believed it.

And when her days to be delivered were fulfilled, behold, there were twins in her womb.

And the first came out red, all over like an hairy garment; and they called his name Esau.

And after that came his brother out, and his hand took hold on Esau's heel; and his name was called Jacob: and Isaac was threescore years old when she bare them [Gen. 25:24-26].

Esau means red and he was red or earth colored. He was the eldest but God had said the elder would serve the younger. Isaac and Rebekah had been married for about twenty years before the children were born. The older one was Esau; they call him "Red," if you please. Jacob took hold on Esau's heel. They call him Jacob, the usurper, for he is trying to become the elder and to take his place. God has already promised that to him. He should have believed God.

ESAU SELLS HIS BIRTHRIGHT TO JACOB

And the boys grew: and Esau was a cunning hunter, a man of the field; and Jacob was a plain man, dwelling in tents [Gen. 25:27].

Now we will look at these two boys as they grow up in this home. Here they are twins, but no two boys were ever more different than these two. They not only struggled in the womb, but they are against each other from here on out. They have absolutely different viewpoints, different philosophies of life. Their thinking is different and their attitudes are different. At the beginning, I must confess, Esau is more attractive than Jacob. But we learn that one can't always judge by the outward sign. We must judge by what takes place on the inside. We learn that in this particular case.

The boys grew. This fellow Esau was a cunning hunter, the outdoor boy, the athletic type. He is the one we would call the all-American boy today. He went in for sports. He went in for everything that was physical, but he had no understanding or capacity, or desire for spiritual things. He was only interested in that which was physical. He represents the flesh.

Jacob was a plain man. I think that you can make of that anything you want to. He lived indoors. He was Mama's boy and he was tied to her apron strings. You will notice that he did what she told him to do. Esau is Papa's boy and Jacob is Mama's boy.

And Isaac loved Esau, because he did eat of his venison: but Rebekah loved Jacob [Gen. 25:28].

Here is the problem in the home. You would feel that under these circumstances they are going to have trouble, and they are. When one parent is partial to one child and the other parent is partial to the other child, you have trouble. That is exactly what took place here.

Isaac loved him because he ate of his venison. Esau went out hunting, and he always got something when he went hunting. He brought home the venison. Isaac liked that, and he liked this outdoor type of boy. Rebekah loved Jacob because he was a mama's boy.

It looks at this point as if Esau is much more attractive than Jacob. He seems to be more of a wholesome boy. This boy Jacob tries to be clever. The fact of the matter is that he doesn't mind stooping to do things that are absolutely wrong, for which God will deal with him. The interesting thing is that although Esau was very attractive on the outside, down underneath he really had no capacity for God whatever. If ever there was a man of the world, he is that man. He is just a physical man and that is all. That is all that he lived for.

Down underneath in Jacob there was a desire for the things that are spiritual. It took God a long time to rub off all the debris that was on top to get down to the heart of this man where this spiritual desire was. But God finally did. Before we are through with our study of this Jacob (his story goes almost all the way through the book of Genesis), we will see that he was God's man all the way along. He didn't demonstrate it until late in life, and we'll come to that.

Now we are told here of an incident that took place in the home there. It could not be called a happy home.

> **And Jacob sod pottage: and Esau came from the field, and he was faint:**
>
> **And Esau said to Jacob, Feed me, I pray thee, with that same red pottage; for I am faint: therefore was his name called Edom. And Jacob said, Sell me this day thy birthright.**
>
> **And Esau said, Behold, I am at the point to die: and what profit shall this birthright do to me?**
>
> **And Jacob said, Swear to me this day; and he sware unto him: and he sold his birthright unto Jacob.**
>
> **Then Jacob gave Esau bread and pottage of lentiles; and he did eat and drink, and rose up, and went his way: thus Esau despised his birthright [Gen. 25:29-34].**

This incident reveals the nature of both of these men. Esau came from the field. He had been outdoors and he was tired. He is not starving to death as some would imply. No one who had been brought up in the home of Abraham would starve to death. There would always be something for him to eat. The thing was that there was nothing prepared right at that moment but this pottage, this stew, which Jacob had made. Jacob is the indoor boy. Evidently he was a good chef.

Edom means red or earthy just as *Esau* does. This man asks for some of the stew, and Jacob saw his chance. He is a trickster and a traitor, and he wanted the birthright.

Let's stop and look for a minute at the value of the birthright and what it means. It means that the one who had it was the head of the house. It also means that the one who had it was the priest of the family. In this particular family, it means that the one who had it would be the one who would be in the line that would lead to Christ. Do you think that Esau had valued it at all? Jacob knew that he didn't. He attached no importance to it, and he didn't want to be the priest of the family. In fact, that's the last thing that he wanted to do.

Sometimes I notice that when a Christian is asked to do something, he may reply, "No, I'm not the preacher." Friend, you may not be a preacher but that does not mean you should not be interested in and work for that which is spiritual. Too many today don't want to show that they are spiritual or even interested in spiritual things. They don't even want to leave anyone with that impression.

That was Esau. He didn't want to give that impression. If anyone would have called him "deacon" or "preacher," it would have insulted him. He didn't want the birthright. He didn't care about being in the line that led to Christ. No one could have cared less about being in that line. So Esau is very glad to make the trade with Jacob. What he is showing here is that the birthright, in his estimation, was not worth a bowl of stew. This is the measure of the value that he attached to spiritual things.

Let us remember that Jacob also was wrong in what he did. God had promised him, "The elder shall serve the younger." The birthright is coming to Jacob in God's own time. Jacob can't wait; so he reaches out to take that which God has promised him. He takes it in a clever, tricky fashion. He should have waited for God to give it to him.

This man operated on the principle that he would do what he could for himself. He thought that as long as he could help himself there was no reason to look to God to perform it. He felt thoroughly capable of taking care of his business. At the beginning he really did rather well as far as the world would measure him. But there came a day when God sent this man off to college and Uncle Laban was the president of the college. It was known as the college of hard knocks, and Jacob was going to learn a few things in the college of hard knocks. But here he is still operating on the principle that he is clever enough to get what is coming to him.

So Esau sat down and ate his stew. He had surrendered his birthright because it meant nothing to him. Nothing that was spiritual meant anything to him. Unfortunately, I'm afraid we have church members like that. They have no spiritual capacity and no understanding of spiritual truths. I believe that the mark of a true Christian is one whom the Spirit of God can teach and guide. It is as if a man today had a very valuable heirloom, let's say an old family Bible which had belonged to his grandfather. Another grandson wants it and offers to give him a quarter for it. So the owner says, "Give me the twenty-five cents because I was going to throw the old thing away anyway." That is the way Esau felt. But we must also admit that Jacob was very clever and tricky in the way he did this.

CHAPTER 26

When I was a much younger preacher, this chapter did not seem to be very exciting. It is quite colorless and uninteresting which is especially noticeable after we have studied a man like Abraham, and an exciting man like Jacob who is to follow. This chapter is about Isaac. In fact, it is the only chapter that is really about Isaac, and it just isn't very thrilling. All he does is dig wells.

In later years I've come to examine these chapters and have found that God has a message for us in this also. In fact, it is a very important message and Paul stated it quite accurately,

> For whatsoever things were written aforetime were written for our learning, that we through patience and comfort of the scriptures might have hope [Rom. 15:4].

This is the chapter to teach some of us patience — I must say that I come under this category. Yet, we would not have you get the impression that patience is all that God wants of us. The Lord also had men like Abraham, like Jacob, and like David, men who were real go-getters and who were aggressive. God can use that also.

> All scripture is given by inspiration of God, and is profitable for doctrine, for reproof, for correction, for instruction in righteousness:
>
> That the man of God may be perfect, throughly furnished unto all good works [II Tim. 3:16, 17].

With that in mind, let us come to this chapter.

Isaac, the beloved son, has the covenant confirmed to him. We find him dropping into the same sin of unbelief as his father Abraham had done. We see him digging wells in the land of Gerar. This doesn't seem to be very interesting, but there is a message here for us; so let us not miss it.

GOD APPEARS TO ISAAC AND REAFFIRMS HIS COVENANT TO ISAAC

And there was a famine in the land, beside the first famine that was in the days of Abraham. And Isaac went unto Abimelech king of the Philistines unto Gerar [Gen. 26:1].

This is now the second famine that is mentioned. You remember the famine in the days of Abraham when Abraham and Lot took off for Egypt.

And the LORD appeared unto him, and said, Go not down into Egypt; dwell in the land which I shall tell thee of [Gen. 26:2].

Why did God say that to Isaac? Well, he had an example before him. His father had run off down to the land of Egypt. This reveals the fact that "like father, like son" sins are carried from father to the son. You can talk about the generation gap all you want. There is no generation gap of sin. It just flows right from one generation to the other. Generally the son makes very much the same mistakes that the father did, unless something intervenes. So God appears to this man Isaac at the time of the famine, and we want to listen now to the confirmation of the covenant that God had made with Abraham.

Sojourn in this land, and I will be with thee, and will bless thee; for unto thee, and unto thy seed, I will give all these countries, and I will perform the oath which I sware unto Abraham thy father;

And I will make thy seed to multiply as the stars of heaven, and will give unto thy seed all these countries; and in thy seed shall all the nations of the earth be blessed;

Because that Abraham obeyed my voice, and kept my charge, my commandments, my statutes, and my laws [Gen. 26:3-5].

You can see that God is merely confirming the covenant that He had made with Abraham. He asks Isaac not to leave the land because God wants to give him this land. He also repeats the covenant about the seed that would come from this line that would have the land. The land is involved in the blessing, but it is the seed that would be a blessing to all nations.

When God says that Abraham was obedient we must remember that God had not given any laws like the Mosaic system. Abraham wasn't under law at all. The important thing is that when God told Abraham to do something, Abraham believed God and acted on it. Abraham believed the promises of God and he acted upon them. That is the demonstration of faith.

We have too many people today who complain that there is no reality. A lady came in to talk to me some time ago who said that she believed, but she just couldn't be sure, and that she didn't feel anything. Such uncertainty! I didn't have to talk to her long to find out that there was no action in her life. She was just sitting in the corner, twiddling her thumbs, saying, "I believe," and then expecting some great something to take place. That just doesn't happen. When you believe God, you act upon His promises. If you would call me right now to tell me that there is a certain amount of money in a bank in downtown Los Angeles and that you have put it in there for me, and I should go down to get it, do you think I would just sit right here the rest of the day? My friend, if you know me, you would know that by the time you hung up the telephone, I would have my hat on my head and I'd be going down there. Faith is what you act on. Faith is something that you step out on. Abraham believed God and God counted it to him for righteousness. God is now telling Isaac that He wants him to be that same kind of a man.

ISAAC MISREPRESENTS HIS RELATIONSHIP TO REBEKAH TO MEN OF GERAR

And Isaac dwelt in Gerar:

And the men of the place asked him of his wife; and he said, She is my sister: for he feared to say, She is my wife; lest, he said, the men of the place should kill me for Rebekah; because she was fair to look upon [Gen. 26:6, 7].

Gerar is to the south. Abraham and Isaac both lived in the south part of that land. Actually, Abraham had come into the land up north to Shechem, but he ended up by living down in the southern part at Hebron, the "place of communion."

Isaac is repeating the sin of his father. God had warned him not to go to Egypt; so he didn't go there but went to Gerar instead. In Gerar he must have seen the men casting glances toward Rebekah, so he asks her to tell them she is his sister. The difference between Abraham and Isaac is that Abraham told half a lie and Isaac told a whole lie. The one he is telling was cut out of the whole cloth.

> And it came to pass, when he had been there a long time, that Abimelech king of the Philistines looked out at a window, and saw, and, behold, Isaac was sporting with Rebekah his wife.

> And Abimelech called Isaac, and said, Behold, of a surety she is thy wife: and how saidst thou, She is my sister? And Isaac said unto him, Because I said, Lest I die for her.

> And Abimelech said, What is this thou hast done unto us? one of the people might lightly have lien with thy wife, and thou shouldest have brought guiltiness upon us.

> And Abimelech charged all his people, saying, He that toucheth this man or his wife shall surely be put to death [Gen. 26:8-11].

Isaac was making love to Rebekah. Isaac had put these people in danger of committing a sin. Now Abimelech had become a very good friend of Isaac. Isaac had the respect of the community just as Abraham had had. Both of them were outstanding men. I mention that here because from the rest of the chapter we might not get the impression that Isaac is an outstanding man.

ISAAC PROSPERS IN GERAR

> Then Isaac sowed in that land, and received in the same year an hundredfold: and the LORD blessed him.

> And the man waxed great, and went forward, and grew until he became very great:

For he had possession of flocks, and possession of herds, and great store of servants: and the Philistines envied him [Gen. 26:12-14].

God is with him, you see. That is the blessing that God promised to these people from the day He called Abraham. It was an earthly blessing. Later on when God put them into that land, He told them He would bless them in their basket; that is, it would be filled with foodstuff. God made that promise good when they were walking in fellowship with Him.

We must remember that He is not promising us that blessing. He has promised *spiritual* blessings to us. We are told that we are blessed with all spiritual blessing, and that is our portion today. But that blessing is on the same terms. It depends on our walk with God. If you will permit Him, He wants to bless you abundantly in your spiritual life today.

Don't miss the fact that Isaac is greatly blessed. His field brings forth an *hundredfold*! The impression is that Abraham was outstanding, and Jacob was also, but not Isaac. Let me say that Isaac is also outstanding. It is true that his birth is tied in with the events of the life of Abraham, and his life is not separated from Abraham either, but let us remember that he is also the important one when he was offered there upon the altar. It is Abraham and Isaac together.

Why should that be so presented? It is because we have already seen that this is a wonderful picture for us. All these things happened unto them for examples unto us. It reveals the intimacy between the Lord Jesus Christ and the Father. Jesus said that whosoever hath seen Him hath seen the Father. In His great, high priestly prayer, He could say to the Father that He had finished the work which the Father had given Him to do. And then He said that His Father worketh hitherto and that He also works. So it is proper that the story of Isaac and the story of Abraham be identified together. Their lives have been intertwined until now and this is the first chapter where we see Isaac standing on his own two feet.

When we find him standing on his own two feet, we find he falls into sin and he doesn't look too attractive. Yet the Word of God makes it clear that he became very great in that land. Yet he does also display weakness and yields to the same sin as Abraham fell into.

The Philistines couldn't stand to see all this prosperity. Abraham had been digging wells in that land and now his son comes along and the wells become his. But he would go out in the morning and find that the wells were all filled up. This was done by the Philistines and, by the way, this is the first mention of the enmity of the Philistines. This led to continual warfare later on in the days of David.

> For all the wells which his father's servants had digged in the days of Abraham his father, the Philistines had stopped them, and filled them with earth.

> And Abimelech said unto Isaac, Go from us; for thou art much mightier than we [Gen. 26:15, 16].

They figured it would be better for Isaac to leave, yet they had great respect for him. This is a part of the life of Isaac that looks like weakness, but it is not. So we find him returning back to that land where his father had been.

ISAAC DIGS WELLS IN GERAR

> And Isaac departed thence, and pitched his tent in the valley of Gerar, and dwelt there.

> And Isaac digged again the wells of water, which they had digged in the days of Abraham his father; for the Philistines had stopped them after the death of Abraham: and he called their names after the names by which his father had called them.

> And Isaac's servants digged in the valley, and found there a well of springing water.

> And the herdmen of Gerar did strive with Isaac's herdmen, saying, The water is our's: and he called the name of the well Esek; because they strove with him.

> And they digged another well, and strove for that also: and he called the name of it Sitnah.

**And he removed from thence, and digged another well;
and for that they strove not: and he called the name of it
Rehoboth; and he said, For now the LORD hath made
room for us, and we shall be fruitful in the land [Gen.
26:17-22].**

This story reveals a real struggle. It is a struggle over water,
and water is a very necessary item in life. You can't have life
without water. You can fly over the deserts of Arizona, New Mex-
ico, and California and see plenty of arid land. Then all of a
sudden you see an area of lush green and wonder what has
happened down there. Water is the only explanation.

I feel the water is a picture of the Word of God. We are to drink
deeply of it. It is called the "water of the Word" and it is for
drinking purposes to slake our thirst, and it is also for washing.
Jesus said that we are cleansed through the Word which He has
spoken. There is a distinction among children of God in any
church today. The difference is the Word of God. You can tell
those who study the Word of God. There is a real struggle here,
friends. It is not easy. I think you almost always have to pay a
price today if you are really going to study the Word of God.

Then he calls the well, Rehoboth. It means "there is room for
us." Before that he would dig a well and they would take it away
from him. He'd move up, dig another one, and they would take
that away from him. He would just keep moving up. This certainly reveals that Isaac is a man of peace and a man of patience.
David wouldn't have done this, I can tell you that. Simon Peter
wouldn't have done that. And if you want to know the truth, Vernon McGee wouldn't have done that. It is a real lesson for us
here. This is especially applicable when we apply it to the study
of the Word of God.

ISAAC GOES TO BEER-SHEBA WHERE GOD AGAIN APPEARS TO HIM

And he went up from thence to Beer-sheba.

**And the LORD appeared unto him the same night, and
said, I am the God of Abraham thy father: fear not, for I
am with thee, and will bless thee, and multiply thy seed
for my servant Abraham's sake [Gen. 26:23, 24].**

God appears to him to comfort him. God appeared to all the patriarchs with the exception of Joseph. He appeared to Abraham, Isaac, and Jacob.

> And he builded an altar there, and called upon the name of the LORD, and pitched his tent there: and there Isaac's servants digged a well [Gen. 26:25].

He goes on again, digging wells. You can always put a well down next to Isaac. You can put an altar down next to Abraham, and you can put a tent down next to Jacob, as we shall see later on.

ISAAC MAKES PEACE WITH ABIMELECH AND DIGS WELL AT BEER-SHEBA

> Then Abimelech went to him from Gerar, and Ahuzzath one of his friends, and Phichol the chief captain of his army.
>
> And Isaac said unto them, Wherefore come ye to me, seeing ye hate me, and have sent me away from you?
>
> And they said, We saw certainly that the LORD was with thee: and we said, Let there be now an oath betwixt us, even betwixt us and thee, and let us make a covenant with thee;
>
> That thou wilt do us no hurt, as we have not touched thee, and as we have done unto thee nothing but good, and have sent thee away in peace: thou art now the blessed of the LORD [Gen. 26:26-29].

Although he almost seems weak in his dealing with the men of Gerar, the king of Gerar was so impressed that he followed Isaac to Beer-sheba in order to establish good relations. The influence of Isaac in that land was not that of a weak man.

> And Esau was forty years old when he took to wife Judith the daughter of Beeri the Hittite, and Bashemath the daughter of Elon the Hittite:
>
> Which were a grief of mind unto Isaac and to Rebekah [Gen. 26:34, 35].

Next time we will see Jacob in his true colors. Thereby hangs a tale.

CHAPTER 27

This chapter has as its theme Jacob and Rebekah conniving to get the blessing of Isaac for Jacob. It is the blessing which Isaac intended for Esau. You see, Jacob wanted the blessing of his father. He knew God had promised his mother that the elder would serve the younger; so the blessing was his already. However, he did not believe God. Rebekah, his mother, did not believe God. Evidently Isaac, the father, didn't believe God or he would never have attempted to bypass Jacob and give the blessing to Esau. He followed his own feelings and appetite in contradiction to the distinct Word of God.

The method Jacob used in obtaining the birthright cannot be supported on any grounds whatsoever. He used fraud and deceit. His conduct was despicable. God did not condone this any more than He condoned the conduct of Sarah and Abraham in the matter of Hagar and Ishmael. God could not use the trickery and cleverness of Jacob. As we shall see, God deals with this man in a very definite way. Jacob had to pay for his sin in the same coin in which he sinned. You will note that as we get into this chapter. This gives us something of a preliminary that will enable us to understand.

Chapter 26 concluded with Esau, who was about forty years old, marrying a Hittite. This was a grief to Isaac and to Rebekah. Now they recognize that if Jacob is not to marry a Hittite or a Philistine, he must be sent away to Haran where Isaac got his bride from the family of Abraham.

ISAAC SENDS ESAU TO HUNT VENISON THAT HE MIGHT BLESS HIM

And it came to pass, that when Isaac was old, and his eyes were dim, so that he could not see, he called Esau his eldest son, and said unto him, My son: and he said unto him, Behold, here am I.

And he said, Behold now, I am old, I know not the day of my death:

> Now therefore take, I pray thee, thy weapons, thy quiver
> and thy bow, and go out to the field, and take me some
> venison;
>
> And make me savoury meat, such as I love, and bring it
> to me, that I may eat; that my soul may bless thee before
> I die [Gen. 27:1-4].

We have seen that Isaac was an outstanding man, a great man.
Abimelech and the Philistines came because they wanted to
make a treaty with him since they feared him. He was that type
of a man. He was prominent and powerful. Here, however, he
reveals that weakness of the flesh. All during his life, Esau had
been his favorite. Jacob was the favorite of Rebekah. Esau was
the outdoor boy who would go out and bring in a deer or some
other animal. He would barbecue it, and the old man enjoyed it.
Now he is very old and he wants to bless the boy. He knows very
well that God has said the elder will serve the younger, but he
bypasses that because he wants to bless Esau. So he tells Esau to
go out and bring in some meat and he will bless him because of
it. What a revelation this is of this family.

Have you noticed the strife in the family since we have come to
this last major section of Genesis? There was strife in the family
of Abraham because of Hagar. Now there is strife in this family
over these twins.

REBEKAH OVERHEARS PLAN AND PLOTS WITH JACOB
TO DECEIVE ISAAC

> And Rebekah heard when Isaac spake to Esau his son.
> And Esau went to the field to hunt for venison, and to
> bring it.
>
> And Rebekah spake unto Jacob her son, saying, Behold, I
> heard thy father speak unto Esau thy brother, saying,
>
> Bring me venison, and make me savoury meat, that I may
> eat, and bless thee before the LORD before my death.
>
> Now therefore, my son, obey my voice according to that
> which I command thee [Gen. 27:5-8].

Rebekah overheard what Jacob had said. Isaac is her favorite; so she conceives this deceitful plan. It is absolute trickery, and it cannot be condoned on any basis whatever. God is recording it as history, but He condemns it. We will see that. Remember the things that are being done here, and later you will see the chickens come home to roost for Jacob. Now Rebekah goes on to say to him:

Go now to the flock, and fetch me from thence two good kids of the goats; and I will make them savoury meat for thy father, such as he loveth:

And thou shalt bring it to thy father, that he may eat, and that he may bless thee before his death.

And Jacob said to Rebekah his mother, Behold, Esau my brother is a hairy man, and I am a smooth man:

My father peradventure will feel me, and I shall seem to him as a deceiver; and I shall bring a curse upon me, and not a blessing [Gen. 27:9-12].

Esau was not only an outdoor man, a red man, but he was also a hairy man.

And his mother said unto him, Upon me be thy curse, my son; only obey my voice, and go fetch me them.

And he went, and fetched, and brought them to his mother: and his mother made savoury meat, such as his father loved.

And Rebekah took goodly raiment of her eldest son Esau, which were with her in the house, and put them upon Jacob her younger son:

And she put the skins of the kids of the goats upon his hands, and upon the smooth of his neck:

And she gave the savoury meat and the bread, which she had prepared, into the hand of her son Jacob [Gen. 27:13-17].

Friends, I can't help but comment on this. She put that skin of the kid of the goat on the back of his neck and on the back of his hands so that when his father would feel him, he'd think it was Esau. She also dressed him in Esau's clothes so he would smell like him! Apparently the deodorant that Esau was using was not very potent. Fact of the matter is, I think he is like the whimsical story I heard. Two men were working in a very tight place. One of them finally said to the other one, "Wow! I think the deodorant of one of us has quit working." The other fellow answered, "It must be yours because I don't use any!" Friends, I don't think that Esau used any either, and I'm not sure he had a shower very often. Even if you couldn't see him, you could smell him.

THE PLOT SUCCEEDS AND JACOB DECEIVES HIS FATHER

And he came unto his father, and said, My father: and he said, Here am I; who art thou, my son?

And Jacob said unto his father, I am Esau thy firstborn; I have done according as thou badest me: arise, I pray thee, sit and eat of my venison, that thy soul may bless me.

And Isaac said unto his son, How is it that thou hast found it so quickly, my son? And he said, Because the LORD thy God brought it to me [Gen. 27:18-20].

This voice was not quite the voice of Esau. Everything else was like Esau. And believe me, this boy at this particular point is typical of pious frauds. You find many such frauds in fundamental circles today. They talk about the Lord leading them. My, sometimes the Lord leads them to do some very unusual things! I find out sometimes that Christian men can do things that the Maffia would be arrested for. But these men can very piously pray about it and say that it is the Lord's will. Believe me, Jacob at this point is a pious fraud. The Lord had nothing to do with this, friends.

And Isaac said unto Jacob, Come near, I pray thee, that I may feel thee, my son, whether thou be my very son Esau or not.

And Jacob went near unto Isaac his father; and he felt him, and said, The voice is Jacob's voice, but the hands are the hands of Esau.

> And he discerned him not, because his hands were hairy,
> as his brother Esau's hands: so he blessed him.
>
> And he said, Art thou my very son Esau? And he said, I
> am.
>
> And he said, Bring it near to me, and I will eat of my
> son's venison, that my soul may bless thee. And he
> brought it near to him, and he did eat: and he brought
> him wine, and he drank.
>
> And his father Isaac said unto him, Come near now, and
> kiss me, my son.
>
> And he came near, and kissed him: and he smelled the
> smell of his raiment, and blessed him, and said, See, the
> smell of my son is as the smell of a field which the LORD
> hath blessed [Gen. 27:21-27].

You can tell that Isaac suspected something was wrong, but
Rebekah knew Isaac very well and she had worked out every
detail.

> Therefore God give thee of the dew of heaven, and the
> fatness of the earth, and plenty of corn and wine:
>
> Let people serve thee, and nations bow down to thee: be
> lord over thy brethren, and let thy mother's sons bow
> down to thee: cursed be every one that curseth thee, and
> blessed be he that blesseth thee [Gen. 27:28, 29].

Isaac is giving the blessing which *he* had received — he is pass-
ing it on. The interesting thing is that it already belonged to
Jacob. God had said that. God had already blessed. God is not
accepting this deception at all. As we watch, we will see this.

THE PLOT DISCOVERED WHEN ESAU RETURNS

> And it came to pass, as soon as Isaac had made an end
> of blessing Jacob, and Jacob was yet scarce gone out
> from the presence of Isaac his father, that Esau his
> brother came in from his hunting.

> And he also had made savoury meat, and brought it unto his father, and said unto his father, Let my father arise, and eat of his son's venison, that thy soul may bless me.
>
> And Isaac his father said unto him, Who art thou? And he said, I am thy son, thy firstborn Esau.
>
> And Isaac trembled very exceedingly, and said, Who? where is he that hath taken venison, and brought it me, and I have eaten of all before thou camest, and have blessed him? yea, and he shall be blessed [Gen. 27:30-33].

Somebody may ask whether venison tastes like lamb or goat. It surely does. I remember several years ago when I was pastor in Pasadena that I went deer hunting in Utah with one of the officers of the church. We got a deer and so we invited the congregation for a dinner just to have a time of good, wholesome fellowship and a lot of fun. We didn't have quite enough meat for all the people; so we bought two lamb legs and cooked that along with the rest of the meat. Nobody could tell the difference and everyone said the venison surely was good.

Now Isaac really sees how he has been taken in by this plot.

> And when Esau heard the words of his father, he cried with a great and exceeding bitter cry, and said unto his father, Bless me, even me also, O my father.
>
> And he said, Thy brother came with subtilty, and hath taken away thy blessing.
>
> And he said, Is not he rightly named Jacob? for he hath supplanted me these two times: he took away my birthright; and, behold, now he hath taken away my blessing. And he said, Hast thou not reserved a blessing for me?
>
> And Isaac answered and said unto Esau, Behold, I have made him thy lord, and all his brethren have I given to him for servants; and with corn and wine have I sustained him: and what shall I do now unto thee, my son?

And Esau said unto his father, Hast thou but one blessing, my father? bless me, even me also, O my father. And Esau lifted up his voice, and wept.

And Isaac his father answered and said unto him, Behold, thy dwelling shall be the fatness of the earth, and of the dew of heaven from above;

And by thy sword shalt thou live, and shalt serve thy brother; and it shall come to pass when thou shalt have the dominion, that thou shalt break his yoke from off thy neck [Gen. 27:34-40].

ESAU'S PLOT TO KILL JACOB AND REBEKAH'S PLAN TO SEND JACOB TO HER BROTHER LABAN

And Esau hated Jacob because of the blessing wherewith his father blessed him: and Esau said in his heart, The days of mourning for my father are at hand; then will I slay my brother Jacob [Gen. 27:41].

In other words, Esau is thinking that his father is old and he can't live much longer. He plans that just as soon as his father dies, he will kill Jacob. "I'm going to get rid of him" was the thought in the heart of Esau.

And these words of Esau her elder son were told to Rebekah: and she sent and called Jacob her younger son, and said unto him, Behold, thy brother Esau, as touching thee, doth comfort himself, purposing to kill thee.

Now therefore, my son, obey my voice; and arise, flee thou to Laban my brother to Haran;

And tarry with him a few days, until thy brother's fury turn away;

Until thy brother's anger turn away from thee, and he forget that which thou hast done to him: then I will send, and fetch thee from thence: why should I be deprived also of you both in one day? [Gen. 27:42-45].

Here, again, we see Rebekah taking things into her own hands. She tells Jacob that she is going to send him away from home. Little did she know that she would pay for her part in this, her sin. She never saw this boy alive again. She said she would send him over there for a little while. But it was a long while and she died before he got back.

We must remember through this story that Jacob was her favorite and that Esau was Isaac's favorite. She wants Jacob to go to her brother, Laban, and that is where she will send him. This is where Jacob is going to learn his lesson. This is where the chickens will come home to roost. Old Uncle Laban is going to put him through school and will teach him a few things. Jacob thought he was clever, but Uncle Laban was an expert at cleverness. Poor Jacob will find he is just an amateur, and he is going to cry out to God in desperation before it is all over.

Notice that she says she will send him for a few days. A few days lengthened to twenty years and during that interval, she died. She never saw her boy, her pet, her favorite, again. One can picture her life during those years when one remembers that Esau is not going to think very much of his mother after this little episode.

And Rebekah said to Isaac, I am weary of my life because of the daughters of Heth: if Jacob take a wife of the daughters of Heth, such as these which are of the daughters of the land, what good shall my life do me? [Gen. 27:46].

Remember that Esau had married these heathen, godless women. Already that was bringing sorrow into the home and even Rebekah was overwhelmed by it. Now she tells Isaac that if Jacob stays there, he will probably do the same thing. She could use this as an excellent excuse to get Jacob away from home because Esau was seeking his life. She has this little conference with Isaac to convince him that the thing to do is to send Jacob back to her family, to her brother Laban. Remember how Abraham's servant had gone there to get her. So now the point is to get Jacob back there to find a wife, but also to get him out of danger. Very frankly, I think that if he had stayed there, Esau would have tried to kill him. However, the way it turned out Rebekah was the first to die and Jacob got back for his father's funeral. But he never again saw his mother.

CHAPTER 28

In the previous chapter we saw Jacob doing one of the most despicable things any man could do. He did it at the behest of his mother. You know, sometimes people excuse themselves for being mean by saying it is because their mother didn't love them when they were little. Believe me, Jacob couldn't say that. Jacob was loved and spoiled. When he was asked to do something that was not quite the honorable thing to do, he did it. He stole the birthright from his brother.

The birthright was already his. The formality of his father giving a blessing wasn't necessary at all. Abraham hadn't given the blessing to Isaac — God had! And it is God who gave it to Jacob. His trickery was not only unnecessary, but God will deal with him because of it, you can be sure of that.

The plan that Rebekah has now thought of is plausible and logical. It probably was the right thing to do in this case. She didn't mention to Isaac that she wanted to send Jacob back to her brother so that he'd get away from the wrath of his brother Esau — that was deception — but she did mention the fact that he could choose a wife back there in her family.

In this chapter we will find Jacob leaving home. He comes to Bethel where God appears to him and confirms to him the covenant made to Abraham.

ISAAC INSTRUCTS JACOB AND SENDS HIM TO LABAN IN PADAN-ARAM

And Isaac called Jacob, and blessed him, and charged him, and said unto him, Thou shalt not take a wife of the daughters of Canaan [Gen. 28:1].

All the way through the Old Testament we find that God does not want the godly to marry the ungodly. That, again, is my reason for believing that in the sixth chapter of Genesis, where it says the sons of God looked upon the daughters of men, it is saying that the godly line married with the godless line of Cain. This finally resulted in the judgment of the Flood with only one godly man left.

Intermarriage always leads to godlessness. I say this as a caution. I recognize that we are living in a day when young people are not very apt to take advice from an old preacher. They wonder what he knows about it all. Frankly, if you want to know the truth, I know a whole lot about this particular matter. I've done years of counselling and have had many, many couples come to me and have been able to watch them through the years. The story is pretty much the same. A young lady or a young man will say they have met the right person, the one they wish to marry. That person is not a Christian. However, they want to marry that person and win him or her for the Lord. May I say this, young lady, if you cannot win him for the Lord before you get married, you will not win him after you are married. May I say this, young man, if you cannot win her for the Lord before you get married, you will not win her after you are married. God forbids the godly to marry the godless. It always entails sorrow. I have seen literally hundreds of cases and I have never yet seen a case where it has worked. Never yet! You can't beat God! God has put it down indelibly all the way through the Word that the godly are not to marry the godless.

Be ye not unequally yoked together with unbelievers: for what fellowship hath righteousness with unrighteousness? and what communion hath light with darkness? [II Cor. 6:14].

The New Testament strictly tells Christians that they are not to be unequally yoked. You don't get unequally yoked by sitting on a platform with an unbeliever, as some critics have accused me of doing! You do it by intermarrying. That's the way you join up with them. And God tells us not to do this.

Arise, go to Padan-aram, to the house of Bethuel thy mother's father; and take thee a wife from thence of the daughters of Laban thy mother's brother.

And God Almighty bless thee, and make thee fruitful, and multiply thee, that thou mayest be a multitude of people;

> And give thee the blessing of Abraham, to thee, and to
> thy seed with thee; that thou mayest inherit the land
> wherein thou art a stranger, which God gave unto
> Abraham.
>
> And Isaac sent away Jacob: and he went to Padan-aram
> unto Laban, son of Bethuel the Syrian, the brother of
> Rebekah, Jacob's and Esau's mother [Gen. 28:2-5].

It is obvious now that Isaac understands that God had given
the blessing to Abraham, that God had transferred it to him, and
that this blessing is to be passed on to his son, Jacob.

If we ask what is the nationality of these people, we would
have to say that they are Syrians. That is what they are called in
the Scripture. Abraham was a Syrian. That is the way to
designate him. Then was Abraham a Jew? Was he an Israelite?
No, he really was not. The nation of Israel does not begin until
Jacob whose name was changed to Israel. Then his 12 sons
become the 12 tribes of Israel. Now it is true that this line comes
from Abraham. He is the father. But he is also the father of
Ishmael and of Midian. So, you see, Abraham is the father of the
Israelites but he is the father of the Midianites also.

ESAU MARRIES MAHALATH, DAUGHTER OF ISHMAEL

> When Esau saw that Isaac had blessed Jacob, and sent
> him away to Padan-aram, to take him a wife from thence;
> and that as he blessed him he gave him a charge, saying,
> Thou shalt not take a wife of the daughters of Canaan;
>
> And that Jacob obeyed his father and his mother, and
> was gone to Padan-aram;
>
> And Esau seeing that the daughters of Canaan pleased
> not Isaac his father:
>
> Then went Esau unto Ishmael, and took unto the wives
> which he had Mahalath the daughter of Ishmael
> Abraham's son, the sister of Nebajoth, to be his wife
> [Gen. 28:6-9].

Now lest someone misunderstand what I mean when I said we
were through with the line of Ishmael, let me say that the Bible

will not follow his line. However, his line will be mentioned as it crosses the line leading to Christ. So here, Esau goes out and marries the daughter of Ishmael. He thinks it will please his father. You see what a lack of spiritual perception he has. The Ishmaelites were as much rejected as the Canaanites or the Philistines.

JACOB ARRIVES AT BETHEL AND DREAMS ABOUT LADDER LET DOWN FROM HEAVEN

And Jacob went out from Beer-sheba, and went toward Haran.

And he lighted upon a certain place, and tarried there all night, because the sun was set; and he took of the stones of that place, and put them for his pillows, and lay down in that place to sleep [Gen. 28:10, 11].

He is traveling north. He comes to a place called — we will learn in a moment — Bethel, meaning the house of God. This place which he reaches the first night is twelve miles north of Jerusalem and his home had been about twenty or thirty miles south of Jerusalem, so that he had covered about forty miles that first day. You can see that he is really hot-footing it away from Esau. He wants to get as far from him as he can, but the farther he gets away from Esau, the farther he gets away from home.

What do you think he was feeling that night? Well, he was very lonely, that is for sure. He was probably homesick. As far as the record is concerned, that was his first night away from home. Do you remember the first night that you were away from home? I certainly remember the first night I went away from home. We lived in the country in a little place called Springer, Oklahoma. They tell me it hasn't done any springing since then. It's still a small place, just a wide place in the road. We had some very wonderful friends who lived down the road. I suppose it couldn't have been over a mile, but at that time I thought it was five or more miles. I've been back there, and I was amazed to find out how close things are together. When I was little, I thought it was all pretty well spread out. Well, these people invited me to come down and spend the night. They had a boy about my age — we were nine or ten, I guess. He had come up to get me, and I shall never forget that we went down together. We had a delicious dinner, a good country dinner, and I enjoyed it that evening with these folks. Then we played hide-and-seek until it got dark which kept me occupied, but every now and then I looked into the darkness and I began to get just a little homesick. Then someone said it was time to go to bed. They put a pallet down in the front room, and I put on the little night shirt that I had brought under my arm, and I lay down on that pallet. Friends, I have never been so lonely in all my life. Homesick! Oh, how I wanted to go home! I rolled and tossed there for a long time. I finally dozed off and I slept for a while, but I awoke very early in the morning. You know what I did? I took off my night shirt and put on my clothes, put my night shirt under my arm and started running home. I didn't stop until I got there. Nobody was up, but I was surely glad to be home. First night away from home. After that, I went a long way from home, but I have never been more homesick than I was that first night.

I have wondered about Jacob. He's actually a man now, a pretty big boy, but I think he is homesick. This is the first time he is away from Rebekah. He's been tied to his mama's apron string all of his life and now he is untied. He is out on his own for the first time.

He lies down and puts stones for pillows. Bethel is a dreary place. It has been described as a bleak moorland. There are large, bare rocks exposed. It is 1200 feet above sea level, in the hills. There are many places out in the desert of California that would correspond to it.

When traveling around in the proximity of Bethel, I was with a bus tour. Others wanted to go other places which to me weren't nearly as important as Bethel. We drove within about a half mile of it and I wanted to walk to it, but the bus driver said we didn't have time. I could see it in the distance and the topography looked bleak and forbidding. Yet this was the high point in the spiritual life of Jacob, not only at this time, but also later in his life. So this is the place he came to, and here he lay down to sleep.

And he dreamed, and behold a ladder set up on the earth, and the top of it reached to heaven; and behold the angels of God ascending and descending on it.

And, behold, the LORD stood above it, and said, I am the LORD God of Abraham thy father, and the God of Isaac: the land whereon thou liest, to thee will I give it, and to thy seed:

And thy seed shall be as the dust of the earth, and thou shalt spread abroad to the west, and to the east, and to the north, and to the south: and in thee and in thy seed shall all the families of the earth be blessed.

And behold, I am with thee, and will keep thee in all places whither thou goest, and will bring thee again into this land; for I will not leave thee, until I have done that which I have spoke to thee of [Gen. 28:12-15].

It was right in that area, by the way, where God first appeared to Abraham after he had reached the Promised Land. Now God is giving to Jacob exactly what he had given first to Abraham. He had repeated it to Isaac, and now He confirms it and reaffirms it to Jacob. He will perform that which He has promised.

You can see how this would be comforting and helpful to a lonesome, homesick boy who really had to leave home in a hurry. He's going to a far country. God promises to be with him and to bring him back into this land. He gave to him the vision of the ladder reaching up to heaven and He spoke to him.

What does the ladder mean? Our Lord interpreted that when he called Nathanael. Nathanael was a wiseacre, by the way. He said, "Can any good thing come out of Nazareth?" Our Lord dealt with this fellow and when Nathanael asked Him how He knew him, Jesus told him that he had seen him under the fig tree.

Nathanael answered and saith unto him, Rabbi, thou art the Son of God; thou art the King of Israel.

Jesus answered and said unto him, Because I said unto thee, I saw thee under the fig tree, believest thou? thou shalt see greater things than these.

And he saith unto him, Verily, verily I say unto you, Hereafter ye shall see heaven open, and the angels of God ascending and descending upon the Son of man [John 1:49-51].

Nathanael was pretty easy to convince although he was a skeptic at the beginning of the ministry of Christ.

Now what is the ladder? The ladder is Christ. God is at the top of the ladder in heaven and He is saying, "This is my beloved Son in whom I am well pleased." God is speaking to man through Christ today. You can't come to God directly. Every now and then I hear in a testimony that somebody will say, "When I was converted, I just came directly to God." My friend, you do not have direct access to God. We have access through Christ, through the grace that we have in Christ. That is the only way that you and I get into God's presence. Christ Jesus is the ladder let down from heaven. The angels of God are ascending and descending on it. They come from Him, the Lord Jesus Himself.

This was first given to Jacob, the usurper. When our Lord saw Nathanael, he said to him, "You're an Israelite in whom there is no guile." There was no Jacob, no trickster, in Nathanael. He was a humorist, a wiseacre. But he was not a trickster.

Now God is going to deal with Jacob, this trickster. He has given him this wonderful, glorious promise, but Jacob has so much to learn. Isn't that true of all of us today? No wonder God has to school us. No wonder God has to discipline us. He scourges every son whom He receives. He disciplines. He did it to Abraham and He did it to Isaac. He is going to do it to Jacob.

Up to now, everything has been going Jacob's way. I received a letter from a couple who had lost their two-year-old boy suddenly one night. Up to that time everything had been going their way. They were church members, but they were hypocrites. So many people are just members of the church, yet they don't know the Lord personally. The Lord has to shake us. He disciplines us and puts iron in our backbone. He puts courage in our lives and enables us to stand for Him. He does this to us, and He is doing this to Jacob. Jacob has a long way to go.

And Jacob awaked out of his sleep, and he said, Surely the LORD is in this place; and I knew it not.

And he was afraid, and said, How dreadful is this place! this is none other but the house of God, and this is the gate of heaven [Gen. 28:16, 17].

This is the passage of Scripture that I use many times in dedicating a new church. "How dreadful is this place!" I think I shock some people, especially when the congregation has come in to dedicate a lovely new facility like we have today. I get up and look around and say, "How dreadful is this place." During the rest of the time I try to win them back to becoming friends of mine by telling them that the place is dreadful only for a fellow like Jacob, a sinner, trying to run away from God. Every house of God, every church, ought to be a dreadful place to any sinner running away from God. It is the place where the sinner ought to be able to meet God, come face to face with God, through the Ladder who has been sent down from heaven, even Christ.

Jacob discovered he was a trickster and a sinner, and actually trying to run away from God. He says, "The Lord is in this place and I didn't know it." When Jacob ran away from home, he had a limited view of God. He thought that when he ran away from home, he was running away from God also. But he found that God was with him here, too. "The Lord is in this place." God told him that He would go with him. Because of that, Jacob says "How dreadful is this place."

JACOB NAMED PLACE BETHEL, "THE HOUSE OF GOD," AND MAKES A VOW

And Jacob rose up early in the morning, and took the stone that he had put for his pillows, and set it up for a pillar, and poured oil upon the top of it.

And he called the name of that place Beth-el: but the name of that city was called Luz at the first.

And Jacob vowed a vow saying, If God will be with me, and will keep me in this way that I go, and will give me bread to eat, and raiment to put on,

So that I come again to my father's house in peace; then shall the LORD be my God:

And this stone, which I have set for a pillar, shall be God's house: and of all that thou shalt give me I will surely give the tenth unto thee [Gen. 28:18-22].

Jacob has a lot to learn and this is an evidence of it. He wants to trade with God. Jacob says to the Lord *if* He will do this for him (and God has already told Jacob He would keep him clothed and fed, would bring him back and would *give* him this land, and would give him offspring), but he wants to trade with God. He says, "If You'll do this, then I'll do that." If God will keep His promise, then Jacob will serve Him.

God doesn't do business with us that way. He didn't do business that way with Jacob either. If He had, Jacob would never have made it back to that land. God brought him back into that land by His grace and mercy. When Jacob did finally come back to Bethel, he came back a wiser man. Do you know what he came back to do? To worship and praise God for His mercy. God had been merciful to him.

Many people even today say they will serve the Lord if He will do such and such. You won't do anything of the kind, my friend. He doesn't do business that way. He will extend mercy to you, and He will be gracious to you without asking anything in return. But He does say that if you love Him, you will really want to serve Him. That will be the bondage of love. It is the same kind of love a mother has for the little child. She becomes its slave. That's the way that He wants you and me.

So Jacob puts up this stone. He is trying to make a deal with God. Yet a great many of us also try to do business with God. Friend, He just wants to become your Father through faith in Christ.

CHAPTER 29

Over this chapter I would like to write:

> Be not deceived; God is not mocked: for whatsoever a man soweth, that shall he also reap.

> For he that soweth to his flesh shall of the flesh reap corruption; but he that soweth to the Spirit shall of the Spirit reap life everlasting [Gal. 6:7, 8].

Probably the title that we ought to put over this chapter is "Chickens Come Home to Roost." In the beginning of this chapter we will see that Jacob begins to reap the harvest of his evil doing. The passage in Galatians is written primarily for Christians, but it expresses a universal law of God in every age. It is true in any area of life. Every child of God must learn his lesson that if he sows to the flesh, he must reap corruption. There is no exception to this rule. If you sow corn, you reap corn. When you sow cotton, you reap cotton. If you sow wheat, you reap wheat, but if you sow tares, you will reap tares.

The Bible is filled with examples of this. Pharaoh slew the male children of the Hebrews and his own son was slain by the death angel. Ahab slew Naboth in cold blood and the dogs came and licked his blood. Elijah came to Ahab and told him that in the very same place where the dogs licked the blood of Naboth, there they would lick his blood. Ahab probably smiled and thought, "Well, I'll just stay away from that place." Yet it was literally fulfilled. David found this inexorable law applicable to his sin. He committed the terrible sins of adultery and murder. God forgave him for his sin. Yet, the chickens came home to roost. He reaped what he had sown. His own daughter was raped and his son slain. Even Paul the apostle felt the weight of this law. He had given his consent at the stoning of Stephen. Later, Paul was taken outside the city of Lystra and was stoned and left for dead.

Jacob is the classic illustration of this inflexible law. Jacob had lived by his wits. He was rather cocky and clever. He had never met his match. As a result, he felt he did not need the help of God. In Uncle Laban Jacob met a man who was more than a match for him. In every way that Jacob had practiced deceit, Uncle Laban outdid him and proved that he was really an expert at Jacob's own methods.

Here in chapter 29, we find Jacob arrives in Haran, meets Rachel and his Uncle Laban, serves for Rachel and is deceived by Laban.

JACOB ARRIVES IN HARAN

Then Jacob went on his journey, and came into the land of the people of the east.

And he looked, and behold a well in the field, and, lo, there were three flocks of sheep lying by it; for out of that well they watered the flocks: and a great stone was upon the well's mouth.

And thither were all the flocks gathered: and they rolled the stone from the well's mouth, and watered the sheep, and put the stone again upon the well's mouth in his place [Gen. 29:1-3].

Jacob had left Bethel and traveled on his journey for a period of time. We are not told how long it took for him to arrive in the land of Haran. We see here the importance of water in that country. It still is a very important item because there is a shortage of it in many places. It must be husbanded and protected; that is why at a certain time during the day the stone was removed from the top of the well, and then everybody watered their sheep. The people would take water for themselves; then the top would be put back on. It is just at the time when they are getting ready to water the sheep that Jacob arrives on the scene. He is as cocky as ever. Listen to him.

And Jacob said unto them, My brethren, whence be ye? And they said, Of Haran are we.

And he said unto them, Know ye Laban the son of Nahor? And they said, We know him [Gen. 29:4, 5].

Oh yes, they knew him. But Jacob didn't know him — yet. But, oh my, Jacob is going to get acquainted with him.

> **And he said unto them, Is he well? And they said, He is well: and behold, Rachel his daughter cometh with the sheep.**
>
> **And he said, Lo, it is yet high day, neither is it time that the cattle should be gathered together: water ye the sheep, and go and feed them.**
>
> **And they said, We cannot, until all the flocks be gathered together, and till they roll the stone from the well's mouth; then we water the sheep [Gen. 29:6-8].**

Here Jacob has just arrived in the land and he is telling them how to water their sheep and what they should do! This is typical of him, by the way.

JACOB MEETS RACHEL AT WELL

> **And while he yet spake with them, Rachel came with her father's sheep: for she kept them.**
>
> **And it came to pass, when Jacob saw Rachel the daughter of Laban his mother's brother, and the sheep of Laban his mother's brother, that Jacob went near, and rolled the stone from the well's mouth, and watered the flock of Laban his mother's brother.**
>
> **And Jacob kissed Rachel, and lifted up his voice, and wept.**
>
> **And Jacob told Rachel that he was her father's brother, and that he was Rebekah's son: and she ran and told her father [Gen. 29:9-12].**

Rachel was a shepherdess who took care of the sheep. This was woman's work in that day. I don't know who told him to water the flock of Laban, but he did it. Jacob is not following anyone's law but his own. He made the rules for the game as he went through life — that is, the first part of his life. He has a tremendous lesson to learn and Uncle Laban is the one to teach him.

It has always seemed strange to me that he kissed the girl then lifted up his voice and wept. It is difficult for me to understand Jacob's doing this unless it was due to his loneliness all the way from the moment he left home. We need to remember that from Bethel he had to go up by the Sea of Galilee, then up into Syria. He had to cross that desert. I suppose he had many experiences along the way. When he arrives at his destination, I imagine he is so welled up with emotion that when he greeted this girl, who was a member of his mother's family, he kissed her and wept. I suppose that would be the only way we can explain it.

You will notice that it calls him her father's brother in verse 12. It actually means nephew. The Hebrew does not make a lot of the distinctions we make today. We've got it reduced down to whether a person is a *kissing* cousin or not, but in that day if you were related, you were a brother. That is the way it is translated here and quite properly so.

JACOB MEETS LABAN AND IS INVITED TO HIS HOME

And it came to pass, when Laban heard the tidings of Jacob his sister's son, that he ran to meet him, and embraced him, and kissed him, and brought him to his house. And he told Laban all these things [Gen. 29:13].

I imagine that he had quite a bit to talk about. I wouldn't be surprised to find that he entertained them at dinner with his story of how he tricked his brother to get his birthright, and how he used trickery to get the blessing, and how clever he was. Probably he told about that night at Bethel too. He told Laban all these things.

And Laban said to him, surely thou art my bone and my flesh. And he abode with him the space of a month [Gen. 29:14].

Laban was convinced now that this was his nephew and he says, "You're my relative, so come in and make yourself at home."

Now a month goes by and notice what happens. Jacob is not working. He's a nephew from a far country and he's come over to visit his uncle. I suppose he felt that he ought to have free room and board there. During that time he's courting this girl, Rachel. At least, he's certainly been casting his eyes in that direction. And I think she was casting her eyes in his direction, too. Now, I can imagine that it was one morning at breakfast when the next incident took place.

LABAN MAKES HIS FIRST BARGAIN WITH JACOB

And Laban said unto Jacob, Because thou art my brother, shouldest thou therefore serve me for nought? tell me, what shall thy wages be?

And Laban had two daughters: the name of the elder was Leah, and the name of the younger was Rachel.

Leah was tender eyed; but Rachel was beautiful and well favoured [Gen. 29:15-17].

This Uncle Laban is clever. Who had said anything about going to work? Jacob hasn't. So Uncle Laban is very tactful and says that he doesn't want Jacob to work for him for nothing. He says that he will pay Jacob. Frankly, you don't live with Laban a month without making some sort of an arrangement to pay your board. Uncle Laban is a clever one also, and now he is going to deal with his nephew.

Here we are introduced to another daughter, Leah. Uncle Laban has been watching this boy, and he has noted that his nephew has become very much interested in his daughter Rachel, the younger of the two. It is explained to us why this happened so we would understand. Rachel is a beautiful girl. Leah was "tender eyed" which is a way of saying that she was not beautiful at all.

In college when we were reading Greek and studying some of the plays of Euripides, when a fellow wanted to say something very nice about his girl, we found in the play that he would call her "cow-eyed." I always laughed about that and thought that I would turn that over in my mind before I ever considered that a compliment. Well now, the next time you meet a cow, take a look at the eyes and you will see they are beautiful. I have never seen a cow that I thought had ugly eyes since I read that play. So when the Greeks thought a woman was beautiful they described her as cow-eyed. But here, Leah, who is an ugly duckling, is described as tender-eyed.

JACOB FALLS IN LOVE WITH RACHEL, AND AGREES TO SERVE FOR HER

And Jacob loved Rachel; and said, I will serve thee seven years for Rachel thy younger daughter [Gen. 29:18].

We find Jacob was quite moon-eyed. So that morning at breakfast when Uncle Laban suggested he go to work, he had something in mind himself. He knew that the boy was in love with the girl so I don't think he was at all surprised at Jacob's answer when he asked what his wages should be. Jacob is willing to work for seven years for Rachel. This man, Laban, is driving a hard bargain. He agrees to it.

And Laban said, It is better that I give her to thee, than that I should give her to another man: abide with me.

And Jacob served seven years for Rachel; and they seemed unto him but a few days, for the love he had to her.

And Jacob said unto Laban, Give me my wife, for my days are fulfilled, that I may go in unto her.

And Laban gathered together all the men of the place, and made a feast [Gen. 29:19-22].

Here is one of the loveliest things that is said about Jacob. Frankly, the only part of this man's life, that is, in the early part of his life, that has anything beautiful, or fine, or noble about it is his love for Rachel. That is outstanding.

You can just see this man working. I tell you, Uncle Laban had him working at many things. He worked out in the cold, out in the rain and in all sorts of weather, but he always thought of that girl Rachel. There she was to meet him after a hard day. He is desperately in love with her.

JACOB IS DECEIVED BY LABAN AND IS GIVEN LEAH INSTEAD OF RACHEL

And it came to pass in the evening, that he took Leah his daughter, and brought her to him; and he went in unto her.

And Laban gave unto his daughter Leah Zilpah his maid for an handmaid.

And it came to pass, that in the morning, behold, it was Leah: and he said to Laban, What is this thou hast done unto me? did not I serve with thee for Rachel? wherefore then hast thou beguiled me?

And Laban said, It must not be so done in our country, to give the younger before the firstborn [Gen. 29:23-26].

Here is a dirty trick. At the marriage ceremony in those days, the woman was veiled, heavily veiled, so that she couldn't be seen. Poor Jacob didn't see the girl he was getting until the next morning. Lo, and behold, it wasn't Rachel. It was Leah. I wonder, at the moment he saw he had been tricked, if he didn't recall something of his own father when he had pretended to be the elder. He deceived his father and that was the reason he had to leave home. You see, God does not approve of that type of conduct. The chickens are now coming home to roost. He pretended to be the elder when he was the younger. Now he thinks he's getting the younger and he gets the elder. The tables are turned now and it has become an awful thing for Jacob. To Jacob it is a criminal thing that Laban has done, but notice how Uncle Laban passes it off. He is an expert at this type of thing. He tells Jacob that there was a little matter in the contract, a clause in the fine print that he had forgotten to mention to Jacob, that was all. It was a custom in their country that the elder daughter must marry first, and the younger daughter could not marry until the elder daughter was married. But Uncle Laban is willing to be very generous in his dealings; so he has an offer to make.

JACOB MAKES ANOTHER BARGAIN FOR RACHEL AND SERVES FOR HER

Fulfill her week, and we will give thee this also for the service which thou shalt serve with me yet seven other years [Gen. 29:27].

This week, you see, is another seven years. Now don't say that this man is going to have two wives and that God approved of it. The record here is inspired in that it records exactly what happened, but that doesn't mean God approved of it. Well,

Uncle Laban is getting his money's worth, isn't he? And poor Jacob is really going to school. But he is taking two wives and he shouldn't have done that. He will be in trouble before it is over.

And Jacob did so, and fulfilled her week; and he gave him Rachel his daughter to wife also [Gen. 29:28].

Poor Jacob certainly had been disappointed. He serves Uncle Laban twice as long as he had originally agreed to. The seven years would have been long enough, but in all he served fourteen years. And now he has two wives. May I say to you, God did not approve of this. Jacob had plenty of trouble in his family from here on, and it all is a result, of course, of his dishonest methods of which God did not approve.

And Laban gave to Rachel his daughter Bilhah his handmaid to be her maid.

And he went in also unto Rachel, and he loved also Rachel more than Leah, and served with him yet seven other years.

And when the LORD saw that Leah was hated, he opened her womb; but Rachel was barren.

And Leah conceived, and bare a son, and she called his name Reuben: for she said, Surely the LORD hath looked upon my affliction; now therefore my husband will love me [Gen. 29:29-32].

This whole story is a sharp contrast to the coming of Abraham's servant to get a bride for Isaac. The servant was looking to God continually for leading. Jacob traveled by his wits and was cocksure and opinionated. The deception practiced upon him by Laban revealed that he was not able to go by his own strength and ability. He needed the leading of the Lord. Just so, the Christian today needs the leading of God and the filling of the Holy Spirit for every moment of the day.

Leah is a sad person, but she becomes the mother of Reuben, the eldest. However, his was not the line that would lead to Christ. The one who is to lead to Christ will be Judah, the fourth son born to Leah. At this point Leah had four sons: Reuben, Simeon, Levi, and verse 35 tells of the birth of Judah. Actually, she

had some of the outstanding boys. Judah is the kingly line —
David was in this line. Then later on, of course, the Lord Jesus
Christ Himself, according to the flesh, came of the line of Judah.
Levi was the priestly tribe. Reuben lost his position as the first
born, you will recall, because of his sin. So the chapter closes
with the blessing of God on Leah in giving her four sons.

CHAPTER 30

When we come to this chapter, we see that God is moving in spite of Jacob's sin. God is not moving because of it, but in spite of it. The theme of the chapter is the family of Jacob and the birth of his sons. Jacob longs to leave Laban, and Jacob makes a shrewd bargain with him.

BIRTH OF TWO SONS OF JACOB TO BILHAH, RACHEL'S MAID

> And when Rachel saw that she bare Jacob no children, Rachel envied her sister; and said unto Jacob, Give me children, or else I die
>
> And Jacob's anger was kindled against Rachel: and he said, Am I in God's stead, who hath withheld from thee the fruit of the womb?
>
> And she said, Behold my maid Bilhah, go in unto her; and she shall bear upon my knees, that I may also have children by her [Gen. 30:1-3].

In that day, a woman was disgraced unless she had offspring, and the more she had, the better was her position. We find here Jacob and Rachel reverting to the practice of that day. Remember that Abraham and Sarah had done the same thing. God is not approving this either. The record is here and it is an accurate record, but it is quite obvious that God does not approve of it.

We have already called attention to the strife that was in Abraham's family. It was also in the family of Isaac, and now we shall see it in Jacob's family already.

The next verses of the chapter tell of the birth of two sons of Jacob by Bilhah, Rachel's handmaid; two sons by Zilpah, Leah's handmaid; and then the birth of two more sons of Jacob to Leah. Then Joseph was born to Rachel and later on Benjamin is born. We'll pause right here and list the 12 sons of Jacob because they are important to get fixed in your mind.

Born to Leah: 1. Reuben
                   2. Simeon
                   3. Levi
                   4. Judah
                   5. Issachar
                   6. Zebulun
                   7. Dinah, daughter

Born to Bilhah, Rachel's maid: 1. Dan
                                 2. Naphtali

Born to Zilpah, Leah's maid: 1. Gad
                               2. Asher

Born to Rachel: 1. Joseph
                  2. Benjamin

Leah bore one half of the twelve sons of Jacob. Each one of her sons had a significant place among the twelve sons of Jacob when they became the twelve tribes of Israel. Levi became the priestly tribe and Judah became the kingly tribe.

BIRTH OF JOSEPH TO RACHEL

And God remembered Rachel, and God hearkened to her, and opened her womb.

And she conceived, and bare a son; and said, God hath taken away my reproach:

And she called his name Joseph; and said, The LORD shall add to me another son [Gen. 30:22-24].

This is the boy who will go down into the land of Egypt. We will follow him later in the book, as he is quite a remarkable person.

JACOB PREPARES TO LEAVE LABAN: LABAN MAKES CONTRACT WITH HIM TO GET HIM TO STAY

And it came to pass, when Rachel had born Joseph, that Jacob said unto Laban, Send me away, that I may go unto mine own place, and to my country.

Give me my wives and my children, for whom I have served thee, and let me go: for thou knowest my service which I have done thee.

And Laban said unto him, I pray thee, if I have found favour in thine eyes, tarry: for I have learned by experience that the LORD hath blessed me for thy sake [Gen. 30:25-27].

Now listen to Uncle Laban. He's not through yet. He learned the same thing that Abimelech, king of Gerar, learned. When Isaac was in his midst, he was blessed. Uncle Laban had discovered that God is with Jacob, and God blessed him. So Uncle Laban asks him not to rush off. He says that he has been blessed, and he'll even raise his wages if he'll stay.

And he said, Appoint me thy wages, and I will give it.

And he said unto him, Thou knowest how I have served thee, and how thy cattle was with me.

For it was little which thou hadst before I came, and it is now increased unto a multitude; and the LORD hath blessed thee since my coming: and now when shall I provide for mine own house also? [Gen. 30:28-30].

Listen to Jacob complaining. He's saying that all he got out of this was two wives. He has two wives, two maids, and a house full of boys. In fact, there are eleven boys. What in the world is he going to do? How is he going to feed all those boys? He tells Laban that God blessed him and prospered him, but that Jacob has nothing for himself.

And he said, What shall I give thee? And Jacob said, Thou shalt not give me any thing: if thou wilt do this thing for me, I will again feed and keep thy flock.

I will pass through all thy flock to day, removing from thence all the speckled and spotted cattle, and all the brown cattle among the sheep, and the spotted and speckled among the goats: and of such shall be my hire [Gen. 30:31, 32].

Jacob chooses the off-breed cattle. These were not the purebreds, by any means. Jacob says that he will take them as his wages.

> So shall my righteousness answer for me in time to come, when it shall come for my hire before thy face: every one that is not speckled and spotted among the goats, and brown among the sheep, that shall be counted stolen with me.
>
> And Laban said, Behold, I would it might be according to thy word [Gen. 30:33, 34].

Jacob is going to separate the animals so they will not be able to breed with the others.

JACOB'S CLEVER BARGAIN PAYS OFF

> And he removed that day the he goats that were ringstraked and spotted, and all the she goats that were speckled and spotted, and every one that had some white in it, and all the brown among the sheep, and gave them into the hand of his sons.
>
> And he set three days' journey betwixt himself and Jacob: and Jacob fed the rest of Laban's flocks.
>
> And Jacob took him rods of green poplar, and of the hazel and chestnut tree; and pilled white strakes in them, and made the white appear which was in the rods.
>
> And he set the rods which he had pilled before the flocks in the gutters in the watering troughs when the flocks came to drink, that they should conceive when they came to drink.
>
> And the flocks conceived before the rods, and brought forth cattle ringstraked, speckled and spotted [Gen. 30:35-39].

There have been various explanations of this. There are those who say this is nothing in the world but that which is superstition. They say it is an old wives' tale and is certainly something which ought not to be in the record.

Another explanation might be that Jacob and Laban *thought* this was what made them ringstraked, but that actually it was the genetic factors in the cattle. Before the separation, the cattle were all mixed together and some would produce ringstraked and speckled but there would also be the pure color. After they were separated, the pure color would probably still produce more speckled ones whereas the chances were less that the speckled ones would produce pure colored offspring.

The next chapter will throw new light on this entire incident. The important thing is that Jacob is using trickery here again.

> **And Jacob did separate the lambs, and set the faces of the flocks toward the ringstraked, and all the brown in the flock of Laban; and he put his own flocks by themselves, and put them not unto Laban's cattle.**

> **And it came to pass, whensoever the stronger cattle did conceive, that Jacob laid the rods before the eyes of the cattle in the gutters, that they might conceive among the rods.**

> **But when the cattle were feeble, he put them not in: so the feebler were Laban's, and the stronger Jacob's.**

> **And the man increased exceedingly, and had much cattle, and maidservants, and menservants, and camels, and asses [Gen. 30:40-43].**

Jacob is quite a trickster. You can see that he hasn't given up his trickery just because he has been tricked. In fact, he is trying to make a come-back. He came there with just a walking stick and now he has great possessions. Jacob's methods reveal that he is still depending upon himself, even after his disappointments at the hand of Uncle Laban. He still has not reached the place where he is willing to cast himself wholly upon the will and wisdom of God.

The believer needs to learn two great truths today. There is no good in the old nature. There is no power in the new nature. Not until the believer has yielded to God and is walking in the power of the Holy Spirit can he produce anything that is pleasing to God and is profitable to man.

Neither yield ye your members as instruments of unrighteousness unto sin: but *yield* yourselves unto God,
as those that are alive from the dead, and your
members as instruments of righteousness unto God
[Romans 6:13].

CHAPTER 31

In this chapter we find Jacob leaves Laban without giving notice. He has that habit, you know, of taking French leave without a goodbye notice at all. Laban takes out after him, pursues and overtakes him. Jacob and Laban then make a contract not to defraud or hurt each other, and they separate in an outwardly friendly manner.

This is a long chapter of fifty-five verses. It contains many facts which have been misunderstood. It reveals something of the character of Jacob. It is a chapter filled with fear, hatred, suspicion, misunderstanding, and bargaining — everything in this chapter point to the fact that Jacob is coming to a crisis in his life. He is approaching "Wit's End Corner." Twenty years of frustration bring Jacob to the point of desperation and decision. Laban has outwitted Jacob at every turn. Jacob met more than his equal in Uncle Laban. Jacob, tired of the endless tussle, longs to be delivered.

There is another side of the coin. God wants to get him out of that land. He knows that the influence there is not good for Jacob and his growing family of boys. Remember, God knows that these boys are to be the heads of the twelve tribes of Israel, and God wants to get them out from that environment and back into Abraham's country, the country that He had promised to Abraham, Isaac, and Jacob. So God is calling Jacob to return.

All of this background and preliminary make this a really interesting chapter.

JACOB REVEALS TO RACHEL AND LEAH HIS PLAN TO LEAVE LABAN BECAUSE OF GROWING ANIMOSITY

> And he heard the words of Laban's sons, saying, Jacob hath taken away all that was our father's; and of that which was our father's hath he gotten all this glory.
>
> And Jacob beheld the countenance of Laban, and behold, it was not toward him as before [Gen. 31:1, 2].

Jacob is now getting more wealth than Uncle Laban is getting. Obviously, Uncle Laban doesn't like this and his attitude is now against Jacob.

> **And the LORD said unto Jacob, Return unto the land of thy fathers, and to thy kindred; and I will be with thee.**
>
> **And Jacob sent and called Rachel and Leah to the field unto his flock [Gen. 31:3, 4].**

God called Jacob to leave and so he is now preparing to do that. He is afraid to talk this over at home for fear some servant or possibly even Laban or Laban's sons might overhear him. He doesn't want them to see him plotting with Rachel and Leah.

> **And said unto them, I see your father's countenance, that it is not toward me as before; but the God of my father hath been with me.**
>
> **And ye know that with all my power I have served your father [Gen. 31:5, 6].**

That is one thing we can agree with Jacob and say to his credit. He had worked hard, but I'm of the opinion that we ought to give Laban credit for that. I believe that Laban got his money's worth out of anyone who worked for him.

> **And your father hath deceived me, and changed my wages ten times; but God suffered him not to hurt me [Gen. 31:7].**

Notice that! Ten times in those twenty years, old Laban had come along and changed his wages. Talk about a trickster! Jacob had thought that buying that birthright for a bowl of stew was a pretty good bargain, but Uncle Laban outwitted him. Poor Jacob. Ten times his wages had been changed. He's frustrated and perplexed and doesn't know where to turn. It is at this time that God has called him to leave.

Let us recognize that we are in a section which God has given to us to minister to *our* needs. We are dealing here with a man who was also a very sinful man in many ways, but a man whom God would not give up. We can take great courage from this. The Lord will never give you up as long as you will keep coming to

Him. He will always receive you. If He will take a fellow like Jacob, and if He will take a fellow like me, then He will also take you.

For twenty years, Jacob has had a sad ordeal with Uncle Laban. He has been having his course in the College of Hard Knocks, and Jacob now wants to escape from all the pressure. Yet, you notice how through all this, he senses that God has been with him and that God has prospered him. The time has come and God calls for Jacob to leave.

Is Jacob beginning to complain to his wives? Yes, I think so. You will notice that he goes on in more detail in the next verses to explain to his wives so they will understand what has happened. I do not think that Jacob was dishonest with Laban here. I think he used legitimate methods which any business man would have used. He was not hurting Laban. God had blessed his animals to the extent that Laban and his sons were very jealous of him and they hated him. You will notice that he goes on to explain all of this, and he tells them why he wants to leave.

THE ANGEL OF THE LORD ENCOURAGES JACOB TO LEAVE

And it came to pass at the time that the cattle conceived, that I lifted up mine eyes, and saw in a dream, and, behold, the rams which leaped upon the cattle were ringstraked, speckled, and grisled.

And the angel of God spake unto me in a dream, saying, Jacob: And I said, Here am I.

And he said, Lift up now thine eyes, and see, all the rams which leap upon the cattle are ringstraked, speckled, and grisled: for I have seen all that Laban doeth unto thee.

I am the God of Bethel, where thou anointedst the pillar, and where thou vowedst a vow unto me: now arise, get thee out from this land, and return unto the land of thy kindred [Gen. 31:10-13].

You probably thought last time that I was not giving a satisfactory answer to what had taken place because I recognized that there are several explanations of the cause of these animals becoming speckled. Actually, I was waiting until we could get right here because now we learn that God was responsible for it. Therefore, I would say that we don't need to look for these natural explanations, although I am confident that God used natural means to do this. God says that He saw what Laban was doing to him, and God is the One who blessed Jacob.

God identifies Himself and brings Jacob's thoughts back to Bethel. This is the place where He appeared to this boy when he was running away from home on his first night out alone. God wants to get Jacob and his boys away from this place of idolatry and heathenism as He previously had taken Abraham out of a home of idolatry.

JACOB FLEES FROM HARAN WITHOUT NOTIFYING LABAN

And Rachel and Leah answered and said unto him, Is there yet any portion or inheritance for us in our father's house?

Are we not counted of him strangers? for he hath sold us, and hath quite devoured also our money [Gen. 31:14, 15].

They are saying that certainly, as the daughters of their father, they should receive some inheritance, and that ought to keep Laban from being so antagonistic. But, friends, old Laban cannot be trusted.

Unfortunately, there are many Christians today who demonstrate in the way they handle their own money and the money of others that they cannot be trusted either. This is, I feel, a real test of an individual. I could tell you some stories that would make your hair stand on end. Christians, and Christian leaders, do things with money that ought not to be done.

For all the riches which God hath taken from our father, that is our's, and our children's: now then, whatsoever God hath said unto thee, do [Gen. 31:16].

I admire these two women. They tell Jacob to do whatever he wants to do. They stand with him, and apparently they feel that their father has robbed them.

Then Jacob rose up, and set his sons and his wives upon camels;

And he carried away all his cattle, and all his goods which he had gotten, the cattle of his getting, which he had gotten in Padan-aram, for to go to Isaac his father in the land of Canaan.

And Laban went to shear his sheep: and Rachel had stolen the images that were her father's [Gen. 31:17-19].

Here is a revelation of something that is quite interesting. Jacob rises up and leaves posthaste again. It is obvious he had prepared for this. He has had practice in leaving overnight. He had the cattle and everything ready to march, ready to get out of that land. Apparently his wives did not have a chance to get many of the things that were theirs. But Rachel stole the images that were her father's. These household gods were probably the Teraphim used by occult and heathen diviners. Modern archaeology has given us new information on the teraphim. At an ancient site near Ninevah, excavations have been made (1925 to 1941) where tablets have been found that illustrate the customs as far back as the patriarchs. Rachel's taking the teraphim from her father was probably much more serious that we had imagined. The possession of those household gods implied leadership of the family, which meant that Jacob was going to inherit everything old Laban had! That is the reason Laban was so wrought up over it. He surely did not want Jacob to get his estate — he felt he had gotten too much already.

Jacob waited until Laban went out to shear sheep. Probably he went quite a few miles away from home because the sheep grazed on a very large area in that day. They still do, for that matter, because it takes a large area to feed them. While Laban is away from home, Jacob just "forgets" to tell him that he is leaving.

And Jacob stole away unawares to Laban the Syrian, in that he told him not that he fled.

So he fled with all that he had; and he rose up, and passed over the river, and set his face toward the mount Gilead [Gen. 31:20, 21].

They are moving quite a distance. Mt. Gilead is just on the east of the Jordan River.

LABAN DISCOVERS JACOB HAS FLED AND PURSUES HIM

And it was told Laban on the third day that Jacob was fled.

And he took his brethren with him, and pursued after him seven days' journey; and they overtook him in the mount Gilead.

And God came to Laban the Syrian in a dream by night, and said unto him, Take heed that thou speak not to Jacob either good or bad [Gen. 31:22-24].

LABAN OVERTAKES JACOB AND REBUKES HIM, HAVING BEEN WARNED OF GOD NOT TO HARM HIM

Listen to Uncle Laban. He's a clever rascal, by the way. He's been coming, breathing out fire and brimstone, and wanting to recover all the possessions which Jacob had taken. He probably wanted to kill Jacob and take back the two daughters and their children. God had to intervene to protect Jacob.

Then Laban overtook Jacob. Now Jacob had pitched his tent in the mount; and Laban with his brethren pitched in the mount of Gilead.

And Laban said to Jacob, What hast thou done, that thou hast stolen away unawares to me, and carried away my daughters, as captives taken with the sword?

Wherefore didst thou flee away secretly, and steal away from me; and didst not tell me, that I might have sent thee away with mirth, and with songs, with tabret, and with harp? [Gen. 31:25-27].

How clever Uncle Laban is, how diplomatic! He tries to make Jacob feel guilty for depriving his family of a wonderful send-off party. He would have had a great celebration and a fond farewell. That's what he *says* but I don't think that is what he would have done. Then he goes on to appeal to sentiment.

And hast not suffered me to kiss my sons and my daughters? thou hast now done foolishly in so doing [Gen. 31:28].

These "sons" would be his grandsons. They are destined to be very prominent as far as the history of this world is concerned.

It is in the power of my hand to do you hurt: but the God of your father spake unto me yesternight, saying, Take thou heed that thou speak not to Jacob either good or bad.

And now, though thou wouldest needs be gone, because thou sore longedst after thy father's house, yet wherefore hast thou stolen my gods? [Gen. 31:29, 30].

Laban finally lets him know that he didn't mean any good for him. It was God who prevented him from doing bad. Now he asks about the stolen gods. Now, actually, Jacob didn't know that Rachel had stolen the gods. When he answers Laban, he is answering about his running away without letting him know.

And Jacob answered and said to Laban, Because I was afraid: for I said, Peradventure thou wouldest take by force thy daughters from me [Gen. 31:31].

Jacob knew that Laban wouldn't have let him take his wives and his family and that which belonged to him.

Now he replies to the charge of the stolen gods. He is sure no one would have stolen then from Laban. You see, Jacob didn't believe Laban. But if you think that Laban believed Jacob, you're wrong. They had absolutely no confidence in each other. It's been a nice, pleasant twenty years together, hasn't it?

With whomsoever thou findest thy gods, let him not live: before our brethren discern thou what is thine with me, and take it to thee. For Jacob knew not that Rachel had stolen them.

And Laban went into Jacob's tent, and into Leah's tent, and into the two maidservants' tents; but he found them not. Then went he out of Leah's tent, and entered into Rachel's tent.

Now Rachel had taken the images, and put them in the camel's furniture, and sat upon them. And Laban searched all the tent, but found them not.

And she said to her father, Let it not displease my lord that I cannot rise up before thee; for the custom of women is upon me. And he searched, but found not the images [Gen. 31:32-35].

He really expected one of his daughters to have them. Rachel's quite a clever girl herself, isn't she? She is the daughter of her father! She had taken them and put them in the camel's furniture, which is the box that went on the camel's back. Then she sat down on them and excused herself to her father. She said she couldn't get up because she didn't feel well that day. All the while, she is sitting on them. What a realistic picture we get of this family!

JACOB RELEASES HIS PENT-UP FEELINGS OF 20 YEARS STANDING

Jacob gets a little confidence now. They can't locate the images, and Jacob is sure that they aren't anywhere around. He wants to rebuke his father-in-law who has come after him. We'll listen to his complaint. Frankly, he has passed the course. He's gone through the College of Hard Knocks and now he is getting his degree.

And Jacob was wroth, and chode with Laban: and Jacob answered and said to Laban, What is my trespass? what is my sin, that thou hast so hotly pursued after me?

Whereas thou hast searched all my stuff, what hast thou found of all thy household stuff? set it here before my brethren and thy brethren, that they may judge betwixt us both.

This twenty years have I been with thee; thy ewes and thy she goats have not cast their young, and the rams of thy flock have I not eaten [Gen. 31:36-38].

He didn't even get his meals. He had to pay for that.

That which was torn of beasts I brought not unto thee; I bare the loss of it; of my hand didst thou require it, whether stolen by day, or stolen by night [Gen. 31:39].

He couldn't even get any insurance. When a lamb was stolen or killed by a wild animal, Jacob had to pay for it. Believe me, this Laban is a hard taskmaster!

Thus I was; in the day the drought consumed me, and the frost by night; and my sleep departed from mine eyes [Gen. 31:40].

He didn't get a vacation in the summer. When the weather grew cold, he still had to stay out with the sheep and with the animals. Many nights he had to watch to protect the flock.

Thus have I been twenty years in thy house; I served thee fourteen years for thy two daughters, and six years for thy cattle: and thou hast changed my wages ten times [Gen. 31:41].

Listen to him. This is what has happened to Jacob. Here is the man who is clever. He thought that he could get by with sin, but God didn't let him get by with it because God has said that whatsoever a man sows, that shall he also reap. Jacob refused submission to God at home; so he had to submit to his uncle. Jacob came to receive a wife in dignity, but he was made a servant because God respects the rights of the first born. Jacob had deceived his father; so he was deceived by his father-in-law. Jacob, the younger, became as the older. Then he found out that he was given the older when he thought he was getting the younger. He revealed a mercenary spirit that displayed itself in the way he got the birthright, allowing his mother to cover his hands with the skins of kids of goats. Later on, we will see that his own sons deceive him in the same way. They killed a kid and in its blood they dipped Joseph's coat of many colors. He deceived his father about being the favorite son, and he was deceived about his favorite son, Joseph. Whatsoever a man sows, that shall he also reap.

Except the God of my father, the God of Abraham, and the fear of Isaac, had been with me, surely thou hadst sent me away now empty. God hath seen mine affliction

and the labour of my hands, and rebuked thee yester-night [Gen. 31:42].

Jacob has had his day in court. He has vented his grievances. Now he is going to leave Laban. They bid each other goodbye and make a contract.

JACOB AND LABAN MAKE THE MIZPAH COVENANT IN FRIENDLY SEPARATION

And Laban answered and said unto Jacob, These daughters are my daughters, and these children are my children, and these cattle are my cattle, and all that thou seest is mine: and what can I do this day unto these my daughters, or unto their children which they have born?

Now therefore come thou, let us make a covenant, I and thou; and let it be for a witness between me and thee.

And Laban said, This heap is a witness between me and thee this day. Therefore was the name of it called Galeed;

And Mizpah; for he said, The LORD watch between me and thee, when we are absent one from another [Gen. 31:43, 44, 48, 49].

The words of this contract have been used by young people's groups and other groups as a benediction. I don't think it ought to be used that way. What actually is done here is that a contract is made between two rascals who are going to quit stealing from each other and work on somebody else! The Lord watch between me and thee is really saying, "May the Lord keep His eye on you so you won't steal from me any more." That is exactly what these men are saying. And after this, they separate. The pile of stones remained at Mizpah as a boundary line between Laban and Jacob. Each promised not to cross over on the other's side.

CHAPTER 32

This is one of the great chapters of the Bible. Have I said this before? Well, there are many great chapters of the Bible and this is one of them. The crisis in the life of Jacob at Peniel is told in this chapter, and Jacob's name is changed to Israel, A Prince with God.

This is a turning point in the life of Jacob, but it is not his conversion. He was a man of God although he certainly had been living in the flesh up to this point. Up to the Peniel crisis, he is an example of the man of God who lives by the ability of the flesh. After the crisis, he is a man of God who will let God lead him.

This is the reason you and I are told to be very careful about judging folk as to whether they are Christian or not. There are Christians who don't act like it, and who give very little evidence of their Christianity. Jacob gave practically no evidence at all. God cannot let Jacob go on like this. He is God's representative, and he is God's witness in the world. He's been a pretty bad witness so far, and God is going to deal with him. God is going to cripple him in order to get him. Just so, the Lord disciplines us.

> For whom the Lord loveth he chasteneth, and scourgeth every son whom he receiveth [Heb. 12:6].

We have already seen that Lot didn't look like a child of God, yet he was. Look how the Lord disciplined him. He escaped the fire of Sodom and Gomorrah, but the Lord put him through the fires of testing. Now this is Jacob's experience.

Jacob got his college degree in the College of Hard Knocks. Uncle Laban was the dean of the school and taught all the classes. He had a graduation and this boy Jacob gave his valedictorian address. It was a pitiful thing. He says it took him twenty years to get his degree, and he certainly worked for it. He says that old Uncle Laban changed the requirements ten times, and always to his disadvantage. That was Jacob's experience.

As an inscription over the chapter before us I would like to write:

> He giveth power to the faint: and to them that have no
> might he increaseth strength [Isa. 40:29].

God moves in on this man and this is now his experience.

JACOB JOURNEYS TO MAHANAIM: ANGELS OF GOD MEET HIM

**And Jacob went on his way, and the angels of God met
him.**

**And when Jacob saw them, he said, This is God's host:
and he called the name of that place Mahanaim [Gen.
32:1, 2].**

God is now dealing with Jacob directly in order to bring him
into the place of fruit-bearing and real, vital service and witness
for Him.

JACOB SENDS MESSENGERS TO ESAU AND PRAYS
TO GOD BECAUSE OF HIS FEAR OF ESAU

**And Jacob sent messengers before him to Esau his
brother unto the land of Seir, the country of Edom.**

**And he commanded them, saying, Thus shall ye speak
unto my lord Esau; Thy servant Jacob saith thus, I have
sojourned with Laban, and stayed there until now:**

**And I have oxen, and asses, flocks, and menservants,
and womenservants: and I have sent to tell my lord, that I
may find grace in thy sight [Gen. 32:3-5].**

Jacob is still clever, isn't he? He just can't let go, even after his
experience with Laban. He remembers twenty years ago when
Esau was breathing out threats against him. Notice that he tells
his messengers to say (of all things), "My lord, Esau," and "Thy
servant, Jacob!" That's not the way Jacob had done it before. He
had manipulated for the birthright and he had stolen the blessing. He had been a rascal but now his talk is different. I guess he
had learned a few things from Uncle Laban. My *lord*, Esau! Thy
servant, Jacob!

And the messengers returned to Jacob, saying, We came to thy brother Esau, and also he cometh to meet thee, and four hundred men with him [Gen. 32:6].

That absolutely frightened poor Jacob because he didn't know what it meant. Esau didn't indicate to the servants his intentions. I suppose Jacob quizzed them thoroughly as to whether they had detected any sign of animosity or bitterness or hatred. I imagine the servants said they didn't. They thought Esau was glad to get the information that Jacob was coming to meet him, and so he started out to meet Jacob. Even the fact that Esau might be glad didn't comfort Jacob. After all, he might be glad for the opportunity of getting revenge! Poor Jacob is upset.

Then Jacob was greatly afraid and distressed: and he divided the people that was with him, and the flocks, and herds, and the camels, into two bands:

And said, If Esau come to the one company, and smite it, then the other company which is left shall escape.

And Jacob said, O God of my father Abraham, and God of my father Isaac, the LORD which saidst unto me, Return unto thy country, and to thy kindred, and I will deal well with thee:

I am not worthy of the least of all the mercies, and of all the truth, which thou hast showed unto thy servant; for with my staff I passed over this Jordan; and now I am become two bands.

Deliver me, I pray thee, from the hand of my brother, from the hand of Esau: for I fear him, lest he will come and smite me, and the mother with the children [Gen. 32:7-11].

He thinks he is really in danger. His brother is coming to meet him; so he divides up the group. He's still being clever — if Esau strikes one group, the other group will have a chance to escape.

Now in his distress he appeals to God. He cries out to God on the basis of the fact that He is the God of his father Abraham and the God of his father Isaac. I begin now to detect a little change in his life. This is the first time I have ever heard him say that he was not worthy of the least of God's mercies! Here is Jacob for the first time acknowledging that he might be a sinner in God's sight.

For years a certain man wrote me lengthy letters. He was incensed that I would indicate he was a sinner, and he told me all the things he had done, and that he'd been saved, and that now he was not a sinner. Well, friend, he is. We all are sinners even those of us who have been saved by grace. As long as we are in this life, we have this old nature that isn't fit to go to heaven, and God is not going to let it go to heaven. That's the reason He had to give me a new nature. The old nature wasn't even fit to repair.

Now Jacob is beginning to say that he is not worthy. When any man will begin to move toward God on that basis, he will find that God will communicate with him. And Jacob makes the interesting statement that he crossed over this Jordan with just a walking stick, and now he is returning with two bands. But he was afraid, and that night he really cried out to God. It was a difficult night for him, and he didn't have a tranquilizer to take either.

JACOB PREPARES PRESENT FOR ESAU AND CLEVERLY ARRANGES TO GIVE IT IN PORTIONS

And he lodged there that same night; and took of that which came to his hand a present for Esau his brother;

Two hundred she goats, and twenty he goats, two hundred ewes, and twenty rams,

Thirty milch camels with their colts, forty kine, and ten bulls, twenty she asses, and ten foals.

And he delivered them into the hand of his servants, every drove by themselves; and said unto his servants, Pass over before me, and put a space betwixt drove and drove [Gen. 32:13-16].

It is interesting that he is generous with his stock now. His tactic is to send out a drove, a very rich gift, for his brother. When that first drove would arrive, Esau would say, "Well, what is this?" The servants would say, "We're bringing you a gift from

your brother Jacob." He'd receive that, then ride on a little
farther and meet another drove of the same size. When he would
ask them where they were going, they would say they were going
to meet Esau. He'd say, "I'm Esau," and they would answer,
"Here's a gift from your brother Jacob." Believe me, by the time
he got down to where Jacob and the family were, he'd be softened
by then.

You see, Jacob had prayed to God and reminded Him that He
had told him to return to this country with the promise He would
protect him. But does he believe God? No. He goes right ahead
and makes all these arrangements which reveal he isn't trusting
God at all.

I'm afraid that is our very position. Many of us take our
burdens to the Lord in prayer. We spread them out before Him. I
do that. Then, when we get through praying, we get right up and
put each little burden right back on our own backs and start
out again with them. We really don't believe Him, do we? We
don't really trust Him as we should.

Jacob prepared these droves and sent them with the servants
with instructions to tell Esau they are gifts from Jacob and that
Jacob is coming behind them.

**And say ye moreover, Behold, thy servant Jacob is
behind us. For he said, I will appease him with the present that goeth before me, and afterward I will see his
face; peradventure he will accept of me.**

**So went the present over before him: and himself lodged
that night in the company.**

**And he rose up that night, and took his two wives, and
his two womenservants, and his eleven sons, and passed
over the ford Jabbok.**

**And he took them, and sent them over the brook, and
sent over that he had [Gen. 32:20-23].**

This is the night of the great experience that came to Jacob.
He came to this very desolate place, at the crossing of the brook
Jabbok. I've been there and I got away from the group purposely.
I took a walk across the bridge that is there now — the United

States had built a very fine road through that area. They built it for the Heshomite Kingdom of Jordan. It takes you into an area you wouldn't be able to see otherwise. It is quite a wilderness area through there. I took pictures of sheep that were drinking down at the brook Jabbok. The crossing there is in a very bleak place right down between two hills. It's rugged, hilly country.

This is where Jacob comes that night. He is not a happy man but is filled with fear and doubts. The chickens are coming home to roost. He had mistreated Esau, and he should not have. God would have gotten the birthright for him. So that night he sent everything that he had across the brook Jabbok. He stayed on the other side, all alone. If his brother came, it might be that he would spare the family and just kill Jacob. So Jacob is all alone.

A MAN WRESTLES WITH JACOB AND JACOB OVERCOMES BY YIELDING

And Jacob was left alone; and there wrestled a man with him until the breaking of the day [Gen. 32:24].

There are several things we need to get straight as we come to this wrestling match. I've heard it said that Jacob did the wrestling. Actually, Jacob did not do any wrestling at all. He has Uncle Laban back of him, and he doesn't mean any good to him at all. He has his brother Esau ahead of him. Actually, Jacob is no match for either one. He is caught now between a rock and a hard place, and he doesn't know which way to turn. Now do you think he wanted to take on a third opponent that night? I don't think so.

Time Magazine, a few years ago, wrote in the sports section of the magazine concerning votes for the greatest wrestler and said, "Not a vote went to the most famous athlete in history, wrestling Jacob." Lo and behold, they got a letter in the mail from someone who asked, "Can you tell me something about this wrestler, Jacob?" They had never heard of him before. Obviously, they had never read their Bible.

Jacob is no wrestler. Let's make that very clear here at the very beginning. That night he was alone because he wanted to be alone, and he wasn't looking for a fight that night.

Who is this One who wrestled with him that night? That is a good question about which there has been a great deal of speculation. I think He is none other than the pre-incarnate Christ, and I have some evidence for it.

> Ephraim feedeth on wind, and followeth after the east wind: he daily increaseth lies and desolation; and they do make a covenant with the Assyrians, and oil is carried into Egypt.
>
> The LORD hath also a controversy with Judah, and will punish Jacob according to his ways; according to his doings will he recompense him.
>
> He took his brother by the heel in the womb, and by his strength he had power with God:
>
> Yea, he had power over the angel, and prevailed: he wept, and made supplication unto him: he found him in Bethel, and there he spake with us:
>
> Even the LORD God of hosts: the LORD is his memorial [Hos. 12:1-5].

The Lord is His name. May I say to you, it was none other than Jehovah, the pre-incarnate Christ, who wrestled with him that night.

> **And when he saw that he prevailed not against him, he touched the hollow of his thigh: and the hollow of Jacob's thigh was out of joint, as he wrestled with him.**
>
> **And he said, Let me go, for the day breaketh. And he said, I will not let thee go, except thou bless me ['Gen. 32:25, 26].**

Old Jacob is not going to give up easily. He's not that kind of a man. Finally, this One who wrestled with him crippled him. And what is happening? Jacob is just holding on. He's not wrestling. He's just holding on to this One. He found that you don't get anywhere with God by struggling and fighting. The only way that you get anywhere with Him is by yielding and just holding on to Him. Abraham had learned that. That is why Abraham said, "Amen," to God. He believed God and God counted it to him for righteousness. Jacob reached the end of his rope and he put his arms around God.

Friend, when you get in that condition, then you trust God. I've read several letters recently from our listeners. One fellow had been on dope, another family had lost a precious little boy in the home, and they had to reach out for help somewhere. My friend, when you are willing to hold on, the Lord is there. He is always ready to help you.

And he said unto him, What is thy name? And he said, Jacob.

And he said, Thy name shall be called no more Jacob, but Israel: for as a prince hast thou power with God and with men, and hast prevailed [Gen. 32:27, 28].

He is not Jacob anymore. Jacob is the usurper, the trickster. He is Israel. Why? Because as "a prince thou hast power with God and with men, and hast prevailed." From now on, the new nature of Israel will be manifest in the life of this man.

And Jacob asked him, and said, Tell me, I pray thee, thy name. And he said, Wherefore is it that thou dost ask after my name? And he blessed him there.

And Jacob called the name of the place Peniel: for I have seen God face to face, and my life is preserved [Gen. 32:29, 30].

After the sun rose over him, he halted upon his thigh. He had seen the angel of the Lord, the pre-incarnate Christ. God had to cripple him to get him, but He got the man. From here on, Jacob will manifest a spiritual nature, a dependence upon God.

There is another young man in the New Testament, a son of Jacob, by the name of Saul of Tarsus. He tells us of his struggle in the seventh chapter of Romans. He couldn't win. Finally he found that by yielding and letting the Spirit of God do what the Law could not do, he could claim the victory. The Spirit of God can perform what the Law can not do in your life. Yielding is an act of the will. That is exactly what Jacob did. Jacob won. He got the victory. He didn't get it by fighting and struggling, but by yielding. Jacob had to be broken before God could use him. And this is the only way that you and I will get anywhere with God today.

CHAPTER 33

Notice how the Lord dealt with him. Jacob refused to give in at first, and that was typical of him. He knew a few holds, and he thought after a while he would be able to overcome. He found out he couldn't overcome, but he would not surrender. So what did God do? You see, God with His superior strength could have pinned his shoulders down, but that would not have pinned his will down. I told you about the little boy whose mother made him sit in his room. After a while she heard a noise in there and asked him whether he was still sitting down. He answered, "Yes, I'm sitting down, but I'm standing up on the inside of me." That is precisely what would have happened to Jacob. He would have been standing up on the inside of him. He wasn't ready to yield.

Notice how God did it. He touched the hollow of his thigh. Just a touch of the finger of God and this man became helpless. But you see, God is not pinning his shoulders down. The struggling and the striving are over, and he is clinging to God.

As we watch Jacob now, we will notice a change. We will not find a total change in a moment's notice. Psychologists tell us that we form habits. We set up certain synaptic connections in our nervous system so that we do things by habit. So this man Jacob will lapse back into his old ways many times, but we begin to see something new in him now. Before we are through with him, we will find that he is a real man of God.

First, we saw him at his home, and then in the land of Haran where he was a man of the flesh. Here at Peniel, at the brook Jabbok, we find him fighting. After this, and all the way through down into Egypt, we see him as a man of faith.

A man of the flesh, then a man fighting and struggling, and finally a man of faith, also characterizes the Apostle Paul. There were three periods in his life. He was converted; he thought he could live the Christian life. And that is where I also made my mistake when I became a Christian. Frankly, I thought that I could live the Christian life. After all, Vernon McGee didn't need any help. I could do it so easily, I thought, but the hard part was that I did not do it. And that is the part where Paul had his problem, you will recall. He continued to do what he did not want to do. He found that there was not only no *good* in the old nature, he found there was no *strength* or *power* in his new nature! Finally we hear him cry out:

> O wretched man that I am! who shall deliver me from
> the body of this death?

And then something happened.

> I thank God through Jesus Christ our Lord. So then
> with the mind I myself serve the law of God; but with
> the flesh the law of sin [Rom. 7:24, 25].

It is through Christ that he had to do all his thanking because from Him his help was going to come. Through Christ. That is the way it is with all of us. We have that old nature, and it can't do anything that will please God. In fact, Paul went on to say that it was at war against God.

> Because the carnal mind is enmity against God: for it
> is not subject to the law of God, neither indeed can be.

> So then they that are in the flesh cannot please God
> [Rom. 8:7, 8].

We cannot please God in the flesh. It is not until you and I yield to Him and let Him work through us, that we can please God. Yielding is an act of the will of a regenerated person yielding himself to God. What a picture of this we have here in Jacob. Remember the Bible tells us that all these things were written for our learning and they happened for an example unto us.

In chapter 33 we meet a new man. This chapter tells us of the meeting of Jacob and Esau. Then Jacob proceeds to Shalem. But this is now a new Jacob.

JACOB MEETS ESAU AND INTRODUCES HIS FAMILY

**And Jacob lifted up his eyes, and looked, and, behold,
Esau came, and with him four hundred men. And he**

divided the children unto Leah, and unto Rachel, and unto the two handmaids.

And he put the handmaids and their children foremost, and Leah and her children after, and Rachel and Joseph hindermost.

And he passed over before them, and bowed himself to the ground seven times, until he came near to his brother.

And Esau ran to meet him, and embraced him, and fell on his neck, and kissed him: and they wept [Gen. 33:1-4].

Jacob wanted to spare his family, you see; so he separated them. I would have loved to see Jacob meeting his brother Esau. I suppose he was a mile from him when he started bowing. He came with his hat in his hand because Esau had 400 men with him. Jacob doesn't know how he's coming, whether he is a friend or a foe.

They are brothers. Actually, they are twins. And they are going to let bygones be bygones. I think God must have touched Esau to change him because he had sworn vengeance and had threatened to kill Jacob.

And he lifted up his eyes, and saw the women and the children; and said, Who are those with thee? And he said, The children which God hath graciously given thy servant.

Then the handmaidens came near, they and their children, and they bowed themselves.

And Leah also with her children came near, and bowed themselves: and after came Joseph near and Rachel, and they bowed themselves [Gen. 33:5-7].

ESAU REFUSES TO ACCEPT JACOB'S GIFT UNTIL JACOB INSISTS

And he said, What meanest thou by all this drove which I met? And he said, These are to find grace in the sight of my lord.

And Esau said, I have enough, my brother; keep that thou hast unto thyself [Gen. 33:8, 9].

For a moment, Jacob thinks his strategy of approaching his brother worked. But notice, it wasn't necessary. Listen to how Esau and Jacob have changed. Esau says that he has plenty.

> **And Jacob said, Nay, I pray thee, if now I have found grace in thy sight, then receive my present at my hand: for therefore I have seen thy face, as though I had seen the face of God, and thou wast pleased with me.**
>
> **Take, I pray thee, my blessing that is brought to thee; because God hath dealt graciously with me, and because I have enough. And he urged him, and he took it [Gen. 33:10, 11].**

This is almost a humorous scene. Up to this time, each was trying to get something from the other. This was especially true of Jacob. Now we find Jacob in a new office altogether. Esau assures him he doesn't need the gift and yet Jacob insists. Believe me, friend, something has happened to change Jacob.

Remember Zacchaeus up in the tree. When our Lord called him down and went with him into his house, something happened to Zacchaeus. He wasn't the same man that climbed up into the tree. He said he would no longer be the tax collector who had been stealing from people and had been dishonest. He wanted to return, not only anything that he had taken in a wrong way, but he wanted to restore it four-fold — and you can be sure that he had taken plenty in a wrong way. What a change had taken place! You could certainly tell which house Jesus had visited.

Certainly there is a change that has taken place in Jacob. Now he insists on giving flocks and herds to his brother for nothing. In that day and in that land if one refused to take the gift which was urged upon him, it was considered an insult. Therefore, Esau takes the gift.

JACOB AND ESAU SEPARATE: ESAU RETURNING TO SEIR AND JACOB JOURNEYING TO SHALEM

> **And he said, Let us take our journey, and let us go, and I will go before thee.**

And he said unto him, My lord knoweth that the children are tender, and the flocks and herds with young are with me: and if men should overdrive them one day, all the flock will die.

Let my lord, I pray thee, pass over before his servant: and I will lead on softly, according as the cattle that goeth before me and the children be able to endure, until I come unto my lord unto Seir [Gen. 33:12-14].

Esau is offering his protection for Jacob as he is returning back to the land. He says he will go before and show him the way. Jacob answers that his family, his flocks and herds with their little ones cannot possibly move as fast as an army of 400 men. So he tells Esau to go ahead with his men.

And Esau said, Let me now leave with thee some of the folk that are with me. And he said, What needeth it? let me find grace in the sight of my lord.

So Esau returned that day on his way unto Seir.

And Jacob journeyed to Succoth, and built him an house, and made booths for his cattle: therefore the name of the place is called Succoth [Gen. 33:15-17].

Esau lived down in the land of Edom. He returns back to his own land, back to his home. However, he leaves a guard to go along to assist Jacob. When Jacob arrived in Succoth he built a house and some barns.

Now let us not pass by so quickly and easily here that we do not pay attention to what has happened. A great change has come over this man Jacob. You see, all of Jacob's clever scheming to present a gift to his brother Esau has just come to naught. God had prepared the heart of Laban not to harm Jacob and so, also, God had prepared the heart of Esau to receive Jacob. Now he has peace on both fronts. Esau did not want the gift of Jacob because Esau himself had an abundance. When Jacob insisted, he took the gift out of courtesy. Both these brothers seem to be generous and genuine in their reconciliation. We have no reason to doubt it. Since Esau is now prosperous, and since he attached no particular value to his birthright anyway, there is no reason why he should not be reconciled to his twin brother.

Now the sunshine is beginning to fall on Jacob's life. Laban is appeased and Esau is reconciled. God had arranged all of this for him. Had Jacob been left to his own cupidity and his own cleverness, he would have come to his death in a violent manner. Before too long Jacob is going to look back over his life, and when he does, he is going to see the hand of God in his life, and he is going to give God the glory. However, the evil that he has sown is yet to bring forth a full harvest. Trouble is in the offing for this man. It is there waiting for him.

Esau rides off to Seir and we say, "Goodbye" to him for the time being. He will be back for the funeral of his father when Isaac dies.

And Jacob came to Shalem, a city of Shechem, which is in the land of Canaan, when he came from Padan-aram; and pitched his tent before the city.

And he bought a parcel of a field, where he had spread his tent, at the hand of the children of Hamor, Shechem's father, for an hundred pieces of money.

And he erected there an altar, and called it El-elohe-Israel [Gen. 33:18-20].

Jacob is sometimes criticized because he stopped here at Succoth and at Shalem and did not proceed on to Bethel. Actually, we ought not to expect too much of Jacob at this time. He's been crippled and he is just learning to walk with his spiritual legs. Jacob builds an altar here, just as his grandfather Abraham was accustomed to building altars wherever he went. The fine feature is that Jacob identifies his new name with the name of God. He called it El-elohe-Israel which means, "God, the God of Israel." This indicates real growth in a man who is just learning to walk.

Let's put it like this. This man is on the way to Bethel, but he hasn't arrived there yet. First he journeys to Succoth. But up to this time, he has not erected altars to the Lord God of his father. Now he has done just that. Now he is becoming a testimony for God.

BIBLIOGRAPHY

Barnhouse, Donald Grey. *Genesis*. Grand Rapids: Zondervan, 1970.

Boyd, Eleanor, H. *The Gospel in Genesis*. Cleveland: Union Gospel Press, 1923.

Candlish, Robert S. *Commentary on Genesis*. 2 vols. Grand Rapids: Zondervan, 1868. (For advanced students.)

Coates, C. A. *An Outline of the Book of Genesis*. Kingston-on-Thames: Stow Hill Bible and Tract Depot, n. d.

Darby, J. N. *Synopsis of the Books of the Bible*. Vol. 1. London: G. Morrish, n. d.

DeHaan, M. R. *Genesis and Evolution*. Grand Rapids: Zondervan, 1962.

Evans, William. *Genesis*. Westwood, New Jersey: Revell, 1916.

Gaebelein, Arno C. *Annotated Bible*. Vol. 1. Chicago: Moody Press, 1917.

Grant, F. W. *Genesis in the Light of the New Testament*. Neptune, New Jersey: Loizeaux, 1945.

————. *Numerical Bible*. Neptune, New Jersey: Loizeaux, 1891.

Gray, James M. *Synthetic Bible Studies*. Westwood, New Jersey: Revell, 1906.

Jensen, Irving L. *Genesis*. Chicago: Moody Press, 1967.

Jamieson, Robert; Faucett, H. R.; and Brown, D. *Commentary on the Bible*. 3 vols. Grand Rapids: Eerdmans, 1945.

Keil, C. F.; and Delitzsch, F. *Commentary on the Old Testament*. Vol. 1. Grand Rapids: Eerdmans, 1949. (For advanced students.)

Kelly, William. *Lectures Introductory to the Pentateuch*. Oak Park, Illinois: Bible Truth Publishers, 1870.

Lange, John Peter. *Commentary on the Bible*. Vol. 1. Grand Rapids: Zondervan, n. d. (For advanced students.)

Leupold, H. C. *Exposition of Genesis*. 2 vols. Columbus, Ohio: Wartburg Press, 1942. (For advanced students.)

Mackintosh C. H. (C. H. M.). *Notes on the Pentateuch*. Neptune, New Jersey: Loizeaux, 1880.

Meyer, F. B. *Abraham*. Westwood, New Jersey: Revell.

————. *Israel*. Fort Washington, Pennsylvania: Christian Literature Crusade.

————. *Joseph*. Westwood, New Jersey: Revell.

Moorehead, W. G. *Outline Studies in the Old Testament*. Grand Rapids: Zondervan, 1894.

Newell, William R. *Old Testament Studies — Genesis to Job*. Chicago: Moody Press, 1950.

Pink, Arthur W. *Gleanings in Genesis*. Chicago: Moody Press, 1922.

Ridout, Samuel. *The Pentateuch*. Neptune, New Jersey: Loizeaux, 1946.

Scofield, C. I. *Bible Correspondence Course*. Vol. 1. Chicago: Moody Bible Institute, 1907.

Thomas, W. H. Griffith. *Genesis*. Grand Rapids: Eerdmans, 1946.

————. *Through the Pentateuch Chapter by Chapter*. Grand Rapids: Eerdmans, 1957.

Turnbull, M. R. *Studying the Book of Genesis*.

Unger, Merrill F. *Unger's Bible Handbook*. Chicago: Moody Press, 1966.

For material on Creation and Science, write to the Institute for Creation Research, 2716 Madison Avenue, San Diego, California, 92116. Henry M. Morris, director.